Seven Principles
of Sainthood

Seven Principles
of Sainthood

Following Saint Mother Theodore Guérin

Mary K. Doyle

SEVEN PRINCIPLES OF SAINTHOOD
Following Saint Mother Theodore Guérin
by Mary K. Doyle

Edited by L.C. Fiore
Cover design by Tom A. Wright
Text design and Typesetting by Patricia A. Lynch

Published by ACTA Publications, 5559 W. Howard Street, Skokie, IL 60077. (800) 397-2282, www.actapublications.com.

Library of Congress Catalog Number: 2008923635

ISBN: 978-0-87946-355-7

Printed in the United States of America by Versa Press

Year: 13 12 11 10 09 08
Printing: 10 9 8 7 6 5 4 3 2 1

Contents

Introduction: The Principles of Sainthood 9

Principle #1: Pray with Saints 13

Principle #2: Trust in Providence 29

Principle #3: Spread the Word 47

Principle #4: Lead by Serving 63

Principle #5: Be Just and Kind 81

Principle #6: Forgive Like Jesus 95

Principle #7: Strive for Humility 109

Conclusion: Following Saint Mother Theodore 125

Appendices

Time Line 127

Mother Theodore's Favorite Prayers 135

Glossary 141

Bibliography 153

Acknowledgments 155

Dedication

This book is dedicated to the Sisters of Providence of Saint Mary-of-the-Woods, Indiana—women religious who faithfully follow Saint Mother Theodore Guérin on the road to heaven. I sincerely thank them for allowing me to have access to their archives and the use of Mother Theodore's letters and journals.

Introduction
The Principles of Sainthood

We know all the excuses for not living exemplary lives. Maybe we think it's not important to refrain from excessive eating, drinking or spending. We say we are entitled to keep material goods we do not need. We spread gossip about our neighbors even when we aren't sure what we say is true. We also tell ourselves we are too busy to go to church, pray, read the Bible, or give thanks for our many blessings. However, we have plenty of time for television, surfing the Internet, and other mindless activities. And sometimes we even may participate in activities that are violent, hateful or obscene without much thinking about them.

Although these activities may appear perfectly acceptable to the general public, the truth of the matter is that we know they are not. How we spend our limited time on this earth is a matter of choice and preference. All too often we choose to follow a path led by human beings rather than the one laid out by our perfect God.

Following Saint Mother Theodore Guérin

This is where the saints can be of great assistance to us. Saints, such as Mother Theodore Guérin, were real people with real problems. They are excellent role models. By examining how they lived and worked through their challenges, we can learn critical life lessons for sanctity.

Saint Mother Theodore was a courageous, compassionate and pious woman who attained great success under difficult circumstances. She came to the United States in 1840 as a French missionary to establish a religious community and schools that provided Christian education to children in the American wilderness.

Potholes riddled her road: Poverty, illness, separation from loved ones, difficult superiors, and outright malice plagued her. Throughout it all, she persevered. She refused to surrender her divine assignment.

Mother Theodore was undaunted by the great hardships she endured because she firmly believed God provides and protects. If she followed the path God laid for her, the outcome could only be victorious. She said, "Pray, be humble, be charitable, and God's blessing will be with you." This is exactly what she did. She submitted herself entirely to the will of God and indeed fulfilled her mission with abundant results.

The seeds she and the Sisters of Providence planted firmly took root. Upon her death, Mother Theodore succeeded in creating an American religious congregation, the first Catholic institution for the higher education of women in Indiana, elementary schools in Indiana and Illinois, two orphanages, and free pharmacies in Vincennes and Saint Mary-of-the-Woods, Indiana. And to this very day, the vibrant community of the Sisters of Providence and the Academy that became Saint Mary-of-the-Woods College continue as a testimony to her providential confidence.

In this book, examples from Mother Theodore's experiences

and quotes from her writings are offered to illustrate the basic principles on which she lived. These principles are commonly identified with holy people. Although timeless, they are not easy, but we too may achieve greatness and holiness by following them on our own road to heaven.

The question you must ask yourself throughout this book is whether or not you have the desire. To be a saint, you have to live like one. Are you willing to live your life by Mother Theodore's principles? Will you, like her:

- ❧ pray with the saints
- ❧ trust in Providence
- ❧ spread the Word of the Lord
- ❧ lead by serving
- ❧ be just and kind
- ❧ forgive like Jesus
- ❧ strive for humility

If so, you are already on the road to heaven.

The prayer of faith will save the sick, and the Lord will raise them up; and anyone who has committed sins will be forgiven. Therefore confess your sins to one another, and pray for one another, so that you may be healed. The prayer of the righteous is powerful and effective.

— *James 5:15-16*

Principle #1
Pray with Saints

Do you believe in miracles? You may recognize little miracles in your daily life, occasions when something works out unusually well for you. But do you believe that you could be completely and unexpectedly healed from a serious illness or disability after a simple act of faith?

Throughout Hebrew and Christian scriptures, we read of many miracles. Women unable to conceive give birth to healthy children long after childbearing age (Genesis 21:1-7). Bread falls from the heavens to feed the hungry Israelites (Exodus 16:13-18). Mobility is restored to the lame (Mark 2:11-12) and vision to the blind (Matthew 9:28-30). Even the dead are brought back to life (Mark 5:35-43).

Miracle of Philip McCord

These unexplained events did not end with the earthly life of Jesus. True miracles occur even today. In fact, at the beginning of this millennium, a man living in a little town in Indiana, the very same town where Saint Mother Theodore Guérin lived, received a miracle recognized by the Catholic Church.

The hardworking, soft-spoken and gentle man named Philip McCord worked as the director of facilities management for the Sisters of Providence motherhouse and Saint Mary-of-the-Woods

College campus that Mother Theodore founded. Phil's responsibilities included overseeing the 1,200 acres and many buildings there. But it wasn't the work that weighed heaviest on his heart in the fall of 2000.

Phil underwent cataract surgery in both eyes. The procedure succeeded on the left eye but resulted in a permanently swollen, droopy and bloodshot right eye with severely-diminished vision. After numerous visits to a specialist in Indianapolis, Indiana, the doctor recommended a cornea replacement. The surgery only boasted a sixty-percent success rate—and a recovery time of more than two years.

The prospect of undergoing another surgery—receiving a cornea from a cadaver, the lengthy therapy without a full guarantee of success—depressed Phil. He couldn't decide how to proceed. Then in early January of 2001, while working at Saint Mary-of-the-Woods, the captivating sounds of the newly renovated organ lured him into the Church of the Immaculate Conception.

Phil sat quietly listening to the music. He told God that he had tried to handle the situation himself. He didn't want to bother God with an unimportant concern in contrast to the many pressing world problems. But he also knew he could not get through this alone. He feared the surgery and asked God for the courage to do what he needed to do.

Then it occurred to Phil to pray with Mother Theodore. "This is your house, after all," he said to her. "Mother Theodore, if you have any influence with God, I would appreciate it if you put in a good word for me."

When Phil left the church, a sense of peace overwhelmed

him. He felt his prayer already answered. He now had the courage to do whatever was necessary to repair his vision. He felt relieved to know that the problem no longer belonged to him: God and Mother Theodore took care of it.

The next morning, Phil showered, shaved, and brushed his teeth. He looked in the mirror, and to his surprise, the skin under his eye no longer drooped. The eye looked clear, but his vision continued to be limited. Phil's wife, Debbie, a nurse, agreed that his right eye looked better, but given its limitations, she made him go to the doctor anyway.

The following week Phil went to his eye surgeon in Indianapolis with a new sense of courage. He felt ready to schedule a date for the surgery, but when the surgeon examined Phil's eye, he was baffled. The doctor looked at Phil's medical chart and back at Phil and then again at the chart.

He asked what Phil's regular eye doctor in Terre Haute had done. Phil responded that he hadn't seen his local doctor. The surgeon asked if Phil had done something else that possibly affected his condition. Phil told the surgeon that he said a prayer.

"Well," said the surgeon, "it worked. The prayer worked."

This confused Phil because his vision continued to be diminished. The eye specialist explained that a mass of tissue remained from the cataract surgery. The mass could easily be removed with minor laser treatment by Phil's local eye doctor; the cornea itself was healed.

Phil went to his eye doctor in Terre Haute. That doctor asked Phil the same questions. He wanted to know what the surgeon or Phil had done since his last visit. Phil gave his doctor the same answer that he gave the eye surgeon—he had said a prayer.

The doctor took Phil into another room and zapped the excess tissue with a laser. Immediately after the treatment, tests showed his vision in that eye to be 20/50. The following week he scored a perfect 20/20. For the first time since childhood, Phil no longer needed glasses.

Word of the cure rapidly spread among the Sisters of Providence. The sisters were like family to Phil. They cared about him and his health. Everyone asked about his right eye and the last doctor visit. When they heard of the unexplained cure, they called it a miracle.

Phil believed in the power of prayer. He realized that he experienced something personally wonderful, but he didn't know very much about miracles. His parents raised him Christian Scientist, and he later became an American Baptist. However, he called himself "somewhat Catholic" because he worked at Catholic institutions for a number of years.

Phil asked many questions of the Sisters of Providence. He wondered why he received such a gift and how he might repay it. The sisters explained that God extended the miracle as an act of love. Phil only had to accept it. No debt needed to be paid.

Extensive verbal and physical exams followed to verify that a certified miracle occurred through the intercession of Mother Theodore. The investigation required, beyond a shadow of a doubt, that no medical explanation for the healing of Phil's eye and vision existed. The miracle was an important—and one of the last—necessary elements in declaring Mother Theodore a saint.

The Church approved the miracle after many meetings of medical and theological experts in the Archdiocese of Indianapolis and Rome. Pope Benedict XVI signed the decree in April of 2006.

Three months later, he gave final approval for the canonization of Mother Theodore Guérin to take place on October 15, 2006.

Canonization of Saints

By baptism, all Christians are called to be saints. We are all to live our life in such a way that gives glory to God. Saints are people who are in heaven after living a life of charity and goodness. The Church recognizes some saints as such, but everyone's life goal should be to strive for holiness.

We pray *with* saints, not *to* them, much like we ask our friends to pray on our behalf when we are in trouble or need. Scripture indicates the value of asking people to pray for us. Saint Paul ended his letter to the Thessalonians with a request for prayers (2 Thessalonians 3:1-2).

We can privately honor anyone who passed away whom we feel lived a holy life. From the beginning of Christianity, the still-living honored and asked for intercession from exemplary deceased Christians. With the approval of the local bishop, the community declared those religious (already honored by the people) to be saints.

That practice changed at the end of the first millennium. From then on, public honor of an individual as a saint required the official approval of the Catholic Church. This certification, called canonization, required a very in-depth and lengthy process.

The first person officially canonized was Bishop Ulrich of Augsburg. Pope John XV declared him a saint in the year 933. By the thirteenth century, a formal process was established for recognition of sainthood. Use of this process continues today and begins with a thorough examination of a person's life, writings, teachings and works.

Two miracles attributed to the candidate's intercession must occur after death. One miracle must take place before beatification when the candidate receives the title of "blessed." The other must occur before canonization when the Church awards the person the title "saint." The miracles indicate the person's powerful and complete connection to God.

When we think about miracles, it is important to remember that our focus is on God, not the saint from whom we requested prayers. We worship God alone. Saint Mother Theodore intervened on Phil's behalf by asking God for help, but only God grants miracles. Miracles are evidence of God's goodness and glory, not the saint's.

The Church offers us saints as role models for holiness. Saints focused on all things God-like and served others before themselves. Mother Theodore said in order to become a saint we must be very submissive to the will of God. We must want only what God wants. She also said that we are obliged to suffer and to not make others suffer.

There are seven official honors bestowed upon a canonized saint. These honors include: the inscription of their name in the catalog of saints and public veneration; inclusion in the Church's public prayers; dedication of churches in the saint's honor; inclusion in the Mass and the Liturgy of the Hours; a day assigned to them in the liturgical calendar; pictorial representation; and the public veneration of their relics.

The First Miracle Attributed
to the Intercession of Mother Theodore

Mother Theodore's road to canonization began when a miraculous healing occurred as a result of her intercession. During her life, many people claimed to have received miracles after she prayed for them. After her death, the town of Saint Mary-of-the-Woods and the Sisters of Providence continued to call on her in a spiritual way. They asked her to talk to God on their behalf.

Sister Mary Theodosia Mug, a Sister of Providence, was one who asked Mother Theodore for prayers. Sister Mary Theodosia received a mastectomy after the diagnosis of breast cancer. The surgery resulted in extensive nerve and muscle damage that left her arm rigid and nearly useless. Of greater concern, the cancer spread to her abdomen. A massive, inoperable tumor made it impossible for her to digest solid food, kneel, or walk without difficulty.

On the evening of October 30, 1908, Sister Mary Theodosia stopped to pray by Mother Theodore's tomb. Her own health issues didn't concern her, rather she asked for the healing of another sister. She wondered if Mother Theodore possessed any power with Almighty God. Sister Mary Theodosia immediately heard a voice within her respond, "Yes, she has." A short time later she heard the affirmation once again.

Sister Mary Theodosia went to bed that evening only to rise within a few hours. To her surprise she found herself making her bed with the full use of both arms. She looked down and noticed her abdomen was no longer distended; her poor vision was also corrected. She went to breakfast, delighted to eat anything she wished.

No sign of cancer ever reappeared in Sister Mary Theodosia. She lived until 1943, thirty-five years after the miracles.

Mother Theodore's Canonization

In 1909, the local bishop of the Diocese of Vincennes, Indiana, granted permission to open the Informative Process of the Cause for the Beatification and Canonization of Mother Theodore Guérin. For nearly one hundred years, every piece of information available on Mother Theodore required close scrutiny. Her life, works and writings were examined in detail.

In 1992 Pope John Paul II granted Mother Theodore the title "Venerable." This signified that she lived the heroic virtues. The heroic virtues include the four cardinal virtues of prudence, justice, fortitude and temperance and the three theological virtues of faith, hope and charity.

In 1997, Pope John Paul II accepted the healing of Sister Mary Theodosia through the intercession of Mother Theodore as a true miracle. On October 25, 1998, he bestowed the title of "Blessed" upon her. This signified her holiness, that she was worthy of honor and veneration. Approval for her sainthood required one more miracle. The miraculous healing of Philip McCord in 2001 fulfilled this requirement.

Formal canonization of Mother Theodore Guérin occurred on October 15, 2006, during a special liturgy in Saint Peter's Square in Vatican City, Italy. A banner with Saint Mother Theodore's portrait draped the front of Saint Peter's Basilica. Sisters of Providence read from Mother Theodore's journals and letters before the Mass, and from Scripture during the liturgy. They also brought to the altar several items pertinent to Mother Theodore's life. These relics included a stone from her birthplace, her rosary and white cross, a letter written in her own hand, a medallion she received for educational excellence, and hand bones from her remains.

During the liturgy, His Holiness Pope Benedict XVI said, "With great trust in divine Providence, Mother Theodore overcame many challenges and persevered in the work that the Lord had called her to do." At the declaration of her sainthood, the massive crowd that filled the square and surrounding streets wholeheartedly cheered. Witnessing this honor bestowed upon Mother Theodore exuded great pride from the Sisters of Providence, alumnae and present students of Saint Mary-of-the-Woods College, past and present students of the Sisters of Providence, citizens of Indiana, and for that matter, all of America, as well as followers of Mother Theodore worldwide.

The following weekend a Eucharistic liturgy of thanksgiving at the Church of the Immaculate Conception at Saint Mary-of-the-Woods marked the momentous event. The Sisters of Providence and campus staff invited visitors to an open house and brunch. Guides stationed at sacred places relating to Mother Theodore's life were available for questions. The celebration coincided with Foundation Day, the 166th anniversary of the day Mother Theodore and her companions arrived at the "Woods."

Life and Works of Mother Theodore

Mother Theodore was the second of four children born to Isabelle Lefevre and Laurent Guérin on October 2, 1798, in Etables, Brittany, France. Baptized Anne-Thérèse Guérin on the day of her birth, she grew up in a happy, faithful home enjoying playful days near the seashore. With the exception of one year of formal education, Anne-Thérèse's well-educated mother taught her at home. It was later said this education exceeded that of the academic and religious studies otherwise available. As a result, her pastor allowed her to make her First Holy Communion at the age of ten, two years earlier than the norm.

For nearly fifteen years, Anne-Thérèse's father served under Napoleon Bonaparte as a captain in the French navy. But on Laurent's return to his family after the French defeat in Russia, robbers murdered him. His death devastated his beloved wife and children emotionally and financially.

Isabelle had already lost two young sons. One child died in infancy, the other in a house fire. Her husband's death was more than she could bear. Isabelle's resulting poor health confined her to bed for years, leaving fifteen-year-old Anne-Thérèse to care for her, Anne-Thérèse's younger sister, Marie-Jeanne, and the home.

Anne-Thérèse grew into an attractive, energetic young woman. Many suitors approached her, but they did not interest her. Her deepest desire was to enter the religious life. In 1823, with Isabelle's improved health and ability to care for herself, she granted permission for Anne-Thérèse to fulfill her own dreams.

Anne-Thérèse entered the relatively new community of the Sisters of Providence in the country town of Ruillé-sur-Loir. On August 18, the new superior, Mother Mary Lecor, accepted Anne-

Thérèse into the order and gave her the name of Sister Saint Theodore. (She would not be known by the title of "Mother" until she came to America and the bishop insisted she be addressed as such.) She served in three parishes in France and far exceeded the expectations set for her. She became a greatly-loved and respected figure everywhere she served.

In 1839, Bishop Celestine de la Hailandière of Vincennes, Indiana, returned to his homeland of France seeking volunteers to work in the United States. On the recommendation of her superior, Sister Saint Theodore accepted the challenge to lead the mission. However, on October 22, 1840, when she first stepped off the carriage that brought her to Saint Mary-of-the-Woods, she did question whether or not she made the right decision.

In the middle of a dense, dark forest, only a dilapidated chapel and a family farm house awaited Mother Theodore and her traveling companions. The welfare of her little group concerned Mother Theodore, and her concerns were not unfounded. The following years brought seemingly insurmountable problems, both natural and man-made. But she met each situation with dignity, perseverance and faith.

Mother Theodore's Devotions

Mother Theodore was a powerful role model for devotion. She placed herself and her mission entirely in the hands of Providence. She prayed the rosary, the Way of the Cross, and her daily prayers. She read Scripture and attended daily Mass and communion. She also practiced adoration before the Blessed Sacrament. In addition to her complete faith and submission to the Lord, she prayed to her favorite saints and angels.

Because of Mother Theodore's great devotion to the Blessed Virgin Mary, she placed herself and her missionary group under Mary's protection. The *Memorare* and *Stabat Mater* topped the list of Mother Theodore's favorite Marian prayers. On her travels across the ocean during violent storms, she often invoked Mary under several of her names including Mary Immaculate and the Star of the Sea.

Mother Theodore lived in an exciting time for followers of Mary. In 1830, in Paris, France, a young woman named Catherine Laboré received a series of apparitions of the Blessed Virgin. Catherine later promoted a medal, known as the Miraculous Medal, designed as Mary instructed. The medal immediately grew in popularity, and devotion to the Blessed Virgin increased as well.

These events intensified Mother Theodore's devotion to Mary. Mother Theodore asked the Mother of God to protect the congregation and schools run by the Sisters of Providence. She firmly believed that all the sisters, their students, and their employees were children of Mary. Mother Theodore often remarked on the evidence of Mary's love for them. They owed everything to her because God channeled graces through Mary to them.

Before a long journey, Mother Theodore wrote in a letter to all the sisters, "Who has ever perished that entrusted herself to Mary? Take her as your model on the way. Often repeat the *Memorare* in her honor for ourselves and for your traveling companions."

This time period also raised great expectations over an important theological decision on the Mother of God. Two years prior to Mother Theodore's death, the belief that Mary was conceived without sin became an official teaching of the Catholic Church. Theologians agreed on Mary's purity for many centuries; the debate over the extent of that purity continued until Pope Pius IX signed the Dogma of the Immaculate Conception, *Ineffabilis Deus*, on December 8, 1854.

The document stated that Mary's immunity from the stain of original sin existed from the moment of her conception. It is believed that God granted this unique privilege to her because she was to bear Jesus Christ, the savior of the world. Only an unmarked, totally pure vessel would be appropriate for the Son of God.

Mother Theodore's love for Mary also extended to Mary's mother, Saint Anne. Mother Theodore prayed to Saint Anne on her voyages to France in 1843 and her return to America in 1844. In thanksgiving for safe travel, Mother Theodore built and dedicated a chapel to Saint Anne at Saint Mary-of-the-Woods. Shells gathered from the Wabash Valley decorated the interior walls. Today you will find a little chapel on that same spot. Although rebuilt in 1876, the chapel walls and altar are decorated with the original shells.

In addition to asking for intercession from Mary and the

saints, Mother Theodore also appealed to the angels. When difficulty with a child occurred, she said a little prayer and asked the child's guardian angel for help. She found this to be an effective method of prayer. She also prayed for intercession from holy people who passed away.

You and the Saints

Mother Theodore looked to the saints as role models and as people she prayed earnestly to on behalf of her special causes. She knew that God provides an extensive network of support through the saints and tapped into them when she required assistance. Mother Theodore asked the saints to pray for her, the sisters, and the students.

The saints are available for us also. The saints experienced earthly sorrow and joy just as we do, and therefore, they understand our needs and concerns. We can rest assured that if we ask for help, if we ask a few of the thousands of holy souls in heaven to pray for us, they will do their best to assist us. The saints will hear our pleas and talk to God on our behalf.

Saint Mother Theodore is now among that group. With her canonization we know that our church investigated and determined that she is a saint. We may confidently pray to her and ask her to pray for us. She lived a holy and righteous life and therefore her prayers are most certainly powerful and effective.

THREE WAYS TO FOLLOW
SAINT MOTHER THEODORE BY

PRAYING WITH THE SAINTS

1. Learn about the patron saint of your name, profession, country or special interest.

2. Pray the rosary; memorize the *Memorare* or the Litany of Saints.

3. Ask your guardian angel or favorite saint for protection before entering your car or public transportation; before going to sleep at night or upon waking in the morning; before making a big decision; or on special occasions or anniversaries.

Trust in the LORD with all your heart,
  And do not rely on your own
    Insight.
In all your ways acknowledge him,
  And he will make straight your paths.

—*Proverbs 3:5-6*

Principle #2
Trust in Providence

Saint Mother Theodore Guérin was a woman of great faith. Her every thought, word and action stemmed from her love for God, her desire to glorify the Lord, and her complete confidence in Divine Providence. Through all of her many struggles, she put her total trust in the goodness and generosity of a loving God. God provided her with the means to achieve whatever mission God expected her to accomplish. She said, "If you lean with all your weight upon Providence you will find yourselves well supported."

To trust in Providence means to have faith in God's wisdom and master design for all creation. The Sisters of Providence's very name indicates the primary principle on which the congregation stands. They trust in Providence completely—trust that God watches over them and sends assistance as necessary.

Throughout Scripture we find references to this principle of sainthood. Jesus said not to worry about what to eat or drink or what to wear. "But strive first for the kingdom of God and His righteousness, and all these things will be given to you as well" (Matthew 6:33).

Mother Theodore met countless challenges. In the midst of horrific storms on transatlantic ocean voyages and immeasurable challenges created by the people around her, she never lost hope or faith in God's love. She placed her life and works completely in the Lord's hands. Mother Theodore knew that God watched over and protected her. She advised her sisters, "God alone remains. Let us attach ourselves to Him with all our hearts and He will take care of us."

Mother Theodore practiced the cardinal virtue of prudence, always discerning the true good in every circumstance. As difficulties arose, she trusted that God had a purpose for presenting each situation to her. She accepted it thoughtfully and thankfully.

In the midst of one very stressful situation, she wrote that she viewed difficulties as being part of the will of God and so submitted to them. Mother Theodore believed God is merciful and generous. Therefore, everything that happened was ultimately for the greater good of humanity.

Dedicated to the Lord

With the guidance of her parents, Mother Theodore dedicated herself to serving God. Her parents, Isabelle and Laurent Guérin, offered their infant to the Blessed Virgin Mary on the day of her birth. In addition, Mother Theodore pledged herself to God on the day of her First Holy Communion and declared her desire to enter a religious community.

Mother Theodore patiently waited for her own mother's blessing to allow her to fulfill her dream of becoming a religious sister. She only desired to spend her life in the service of God. She entered the Sisters of Providence novitiate in Ruillé-sur-Loir, France, on August 18, 1823. (The novitiate is a period of preparation and formation of religious instruction during which the novice—the woman entering the community—and her superiors determine whether or not she is suitable for religious life.)

In January of 1825, Mother Theodore's superior, Mother Mary Lecor, sent her to teach in the town of Preuilly-sur-Claise. France desperately needed religious women, but little time was available to train them to teach and evangelize. Most of their preparation resulted from on-site experience at the mission.

Mother Theodore professed her first vows on September 8, 1825. She received the religious habit at that time. By professing those vows, she promised to observe poverty, chastity and obedience while in the novitiate. Sisters of Providence also promised to teach and care for the sick and poor.

Six years later, on September 5, 1831, Mother Theodore professed her perpetual vows. She promised to observe her vows forever. Her superior then assigned her to the large and difficult parish of Saint Aubin at Rennes.

Dedicating herself to God and God's work was never a challenge for Mother Theodore. She felt bound to the commitment she made to God on her First Holy Communion day. The formality of professing her vows and the official tie to the community of the Sisters of Providence made the only difference.

A Prayerful Life

The majority of Mother Theodore's letters and journal entries that we have today contain reference to prayer. She regularly assured her friends, family, and especially the sisters that she prayed for them. She also asked for their prayers in return.

Occasionally she wrote a prayer and included it in a letter. Following is a beautiful blessing she addressed to the sisters in

Jasper, Indiana. The letter dated March 20, 1843 reads:

> *May our Savior Jesus Christ fill your hearts with His love;*
> *may the blessed Virgin Mary, our sweet Mother, have you in*
> *her holy keeping; may the angels guard and direct you.*

Mother Theodore wrote numerous prayers of thanksgiving. She realized God's generosity and appreciated every gift, no matter how small. She encouraged the sisters and her friends to join her in giving thanks. She said committing themselves more perfectly to God—and the mission to which God pointed them —proved their gratitude.

At the onset of Mother Theodore and the sisters' journey to the United States, she felt that although they made the sacrifice for God, God already repaid them for their efforts. Abundance filled their lives. They couldn't do anything less than recognize the goodness of the Lord in all that they had and in the opportunities that lay ahead of them.

The natural wonders inspired Mother Theodore in particular. On her ocean voyage the sunsets, variety of wildlife, and creatures of the sea amazed her. She marveled at the aurora borealis and wrote of seeing whales on more than one occasion. She saw all this as proof of God's glory and magnificence. When the weather calmed, she would go on deck and thank God for all the splendor of creation. "I love to consider the care of God's Providence, which extends even to the little fishes," she said.

She also saw God's glory in the beauty of the Indiana forests. She admired the birds and animals, the trees in springtime bloom, the rolling hills and rivers. She wrote of the beauty of the magnolia, the dogwood and catalpa, the hummingbird, stag, and "serpents" of all colors.

However, the Blessed Sacrament captured Mother Theodore's greatest devotion. When arriving at any destination, she knelt before the tabernacle or monstrance (the sacred vessel used for the exposition of the Blessed Sacrament) before speaking to anyone or doing anything else. Giving thanks and praise to God was always her first priority.

As a teacher and evangelizer, witnessing the faith and devotion in others pleased Mother Theodore. On her way across the country she observed and admired the piety of the Americans. She identified them with the spirit of the Christians of the primitive Church. She noted their great charity, the love of hospitality that Saint Paul recommended, an ardent zeal for the Gospel, and all the virtues of the Fathers of the Faith.

Mother Theodore found the piety of the parish in Jasper, Indiana, remarkable. The German community walked seven to ten miles to attend Mass, processing double file and singing hymns all the way. After a long service, with homilies in both English and German, the congregation marched back to their homes, again singing sacred songs and praising God.

Mother Theodore found it most rewarding to watch the growth of faith and devotion of the Sisters of Providence. The ceremonies of the novices never ceased to be an emotional event for her. The incoming American sisters warmed her heart. She said they were, "so occupied with the affairs of their souls, with the desire of pleasing God, of making sacrifices to Him."

Test of Faith

The true test of faith always comes during tough times. Mother Theodore did not live a privileged life. She received few advantages or comforts and countless challenges and losses confronted her. Throughout it all, her faith in Providence remained strong.

Many of Mother Theodore's letters to the sisters, and her journal entries, dealt with suffering. She believed that God's mercy and generosity is evident even in the most desperate of times. She gave thanks for painful events because she believed they served a purpose in the divine plan. She met her tribulations with perseverance and courage, and her faith grew stronger with time.

Mother Theodore experienced separation from loved ones on several occasions. She lost two brothers during her childhood and her father while she was only a teenager. She also missed her mother and sisters when she first entered the religious community. Certainly, leaving her home country of France resulted in the most severe separation. She knew she most likely would never see her family and friends again.

Mother Theodore accepted this sacrifice as part of the life of a Christian and especially that of a religious, a woman who committed to a life of God's work. She trusted God to provide her with people to love and to be loved by wherever she may be. More importantly, her love for God filled her heart.

Missionaries often venture through and into dangerous environments. Mother Theodore's voyage of 1840 to America was a grueling experience. Violent storms tossed passengers and crew about like rag dolls. Some passengers screamed in fear, but Mother Theodore and her five companions calmly prayed throughout the trip, regardless of the conditions.

At one point, a fearful rabbi approached Mother Theodore and the sisters. When he saw the women, their calmness astonished him. He asked how they could be so oblivious to the terror surrounding them. Mother Theodore said they prayed, asked the Lord for forgiveness, and trusted the outcome to be what God believed best for them.

In her journal, she wrote that the thought of dying in the turbulent storms aboard the ship did not frighten her. She only feared for her companions. In the event of her death, she hoped not to put them through the experience of burying her body at sea.

Mother Theodore's first indication of the difficulties she faced in her missionary work in the New World occurred when she finally docked on American soil. Her superior, Mother Mary, sent money ahead to the bishop of Vincennes, Indiana, for the use of the Sisters of Providence. The bishop or an escort was to be waiting for them and accompany the sisters to their new home. However, not only did the bishop fail to meet them upon arrival, he did not see them until they arrived in Vincennes. Nor did he send anyone else to meet them.

Travel across the country, especially for single women in those days, was not a safe endeavor. Bandits preyed on passengers in coaches. Officials advised the women not to embark on a journey without a male escort. The language barrier put the Sisters of Providence at an additional disadvantage. They spoke French and little English.

Mother Theodore did not lose hope that God would assist them, and Providence did intervene with priests, religious and laypeople who eagerly helped them along their journey to Indiana. A physician from the Custom House, Doctor Sidney A. Doane, reached out to them with refreshments and friendship. He introduced them to a priest, Father Varella, and a layperson, Mrs. Parmentier, who welcomed them and cared for all their needs.

These two in turn connected Mother Theodore and her companions with other helpful people, such as the Sisters of Charity in Philadelphia and Baltimore, who opened their homes and offered hospitality to the Sisters of Providence. The bishop of Philadelphia even introduced the little group to a French priest from Canada, the Reverend William Chartier, who was going to Vincennes and offered to escort them all the way to Indiana.

After Mother Theodore and the sisters arrived at Saint Mary-of-the-Woods, they encountered new troubles. No one found prairie life in the early to mid-1800s easy: Americans struggled for survival. They battled the elements while establishing a homestead and raising enough crops and livestock to feed their families. The clergy and religious were no exception. They also experienced great poverty during those times.

Fire hazards caused constant concern. Heat, cooking and light required the use of controlled fire, but sparks, smoldering cinders, and flammable items left too close to flames often resulted in fires that ran amiss. Many of these fires ended in death, especially among young children.

Several tragic fires occurred at Saint Mary-of-the-Woods in the early years. The fire of October 2, 1842, is not thought to have been an accident. It was Mother Theodore's forty-second birthday. While talking with a novice in the main house, she heard shouting. One of the small houses on the property was in flames.

The fire quickly spread to the barn.

Workmen did their best to prevent further devastation, but within no time, fire devoured all the winter feed, the entire supply of flour, other provisions, and farm implements. Mother Theodore simply looked at the charred remains and went back into her house. She returned with hot wine to serve to the workers and neighbors who had risked their own safety to extinguish the flames.

They never learned the cause of the fire. A break in the fence suggested the possibility that vandals deliberately set the fire while everyone attended Mass. It wouldn't have been the first time anti-Catholic groups torched a religious institution.

The exceptional harvest gathered that year would have eased them through the coming winter and spring. That possibility went up in the flames. They also lost the necessary equipment for the next spring's planting. It took many years before the Sisters of Providence recovered from the loss.

Trust God, Only God

Mother Theodore learned early in life that human beings would let her down. Her only salvation came from the Almighty One. Repeatedly, she gave this advice to others. She said to trust God, put all your hope in God, and Providence never fails.

Those in positions to assist and protect Mother Theodore often failed to do so. She should have been able to rely on her own mother, superior general, first chaplain, and first bishop in America. She soon found that she could not. They all proved untrustworthy, to one degree or another. God alone guided her.

Her first such experience occurred with her father's death

and the subsequent emotional breakdown of her mother. Not only was Mother Theodore required to assume the position of caretaker to her own mother and sister, but she also lacked a parent to care for her. Not quite fifteen years old, she became the woman of the house. The family income came entirely from her work as a seamstress. Mother Theodore handled this responsibility with ability, dignity and compassion. She relied on her limited experience and faith in the Lord, caring for her family in this way for ten years.

Two members of the clergy possibly created her most difficult relationships. The first chaplain at Saint Mary-of-the-Woods, Reverend Stanislaus Buteux, tried to control the little religious community of the Sisters of Providence. He repeatedly worked to undermine Mother Theodore's success as superior of the new motherhouse.

Although Bishop de la Hailandière replaced the chaplain because of the priest's authoritarian attitude, the bishop became even more controlling than Father Buteux. Bishop de la Hailandière sometimes treated the sisters thoughtfully, showing them support and care. However, most often he controlled and oppressed Mother Theodore and the sisters. He wanted jurisdiction over every decision regarding them, no matter how small.

Needless to say, this put Mother Theodore in a terrible position. As leader of the community, her responsibility required her to protect the sisters and prepare them for their mission. She had to stand up to the bishop. She agonized over how this could be done while continuing to award the bishop the respect due his position.

Mother Theodore put her trust in Providence. She wrote

to her friend and mentor in France, Bishop Bouvier. "I feel certain that nothing will happen except what God will permit. He has protected us with so much love until the present day that I should consider it a crime to doubt His mercy now."

For nearly seven years Mother Theodore dealt with the bishop's erratic behavior. God finally did answer her most desperate prayers. She received word in 1846 that the pope accepted Bishop de la Hailandière's resignation. Although she respected the bishop, he caused her severe and unwarranted stress. It relieved her to know that quieter days were in the sisters' futures.

The new bishop, John Stephen Bazin, was consecrated to the Diocese of Vincennes on October 24, 1847. Bishop Bazin supported, encouraged and cared for the Sisters of Providence. Unfortunately, he only lived for six more months. No sooner did he envelop the sisters with a sense of peace that they had not experienced since their arrival in America, than he passed away from an infectious disease.

Bishop Bazin's death came as a shock and great disappointment to the sisters. Yet, Mother Theodore's faith remained unshaken. She trusted in God's Almighty plan for them. She told the sisters to submit with love to the will of God. "He has always protected us; if we love Him, He will never abandon us."

The Right Reverend Maurice de Saint Palais replaced Bishop Bazin on his consecration on January 14, 1849. Already a friend to Mother Theodore, he showed kindness and support to the community long before becoming bishop. Mother Theodore told Bishop Bouvier that Bishop de Saint Palais made their past trials disappear completely. She appreciated his wisdom and the liberty he awarded her to make her own decisions.

Mother Theodore persevered and survived these difficult situations because of her faith in Providence, but this is not to say that she did not experience frustration or sorrow. Most of her years in America proved extremely problematic. She had reason to feel discouraged from time to time. On February 23, 1843, she wrote to Bishop Bouvier, "This habitual state of calm, it is true, has from time to time its tempests. I am sometimes so depressed, so disheartened that I feel inclined to excessive sadness. In these moments I often felt I should be glad to die; but immediately thinking of my sisters, I have been ashamed of my cowardice and have asked God's pardon."

As women religious, Mother Theodore and the sisters entered the community to accomplish God's will in God's way. Sacrifices and hardships were to be expected. Regardless of the level of emotional or physical pain she or anyone else suffered, Mother Theodore said not to dwell upon these difficulties. She advised her sisters that sadness is very hurtful for the soul and body. She firmly added, "Do not indulge in it."

With each passing day Mother Theodore saw that the religious spirit among the Sisters of Providence of Saint Mary-of-the-Woods became increasingly more solid. The women's spiritual growth gave her hope. She did not doubt that if they were good religious, all would be well. "If He be with us, who shall be against us?"

Chronic Illness

Mother Theodore experienced her most constant difficulties with her chronic health problems. While a novice, she contracted a serious illness, most likely smallpox. She was so ill that at one point her mother superior doubted she would survive.

The unsophisticated medical treatment available in the early nineteenth century finally cured her, but it permanently damaged her intestines. From then on she no longer could digest solid food, making it difficult for her to consume adequate nutrition. Her immune system perpetually teetered on a fragile balance, and stress easily tipped the scale, leaving her susceptible to contagious disease.

Once she recovered from her initial illness, Mother Theodore's health remained poor but fairly stable—until her sea voyage to America. The ship, the *Cincinnati*, lacked any form of comfort or sanitation. The sisters found the rooms cramped and stuffy. Meals consisted of basic soup. No spoons were available, so they ate with a fork and the blade of the knife. Clean water was nowhere to be found.

The turbulent ocean resulted in seasickness for most passengers including Mother Theodore and her companions. The sisters struggled to care for one another. In addition, Mother Theodore developed a high fever and had difficulty regaining her strength.

Once on land, her health remained fragile. During their first Christmas at Saint Mary-of-the-Woods, Mother Theodore came down with a violent headache and fever, an illness referred to then as "brain fever." The sisters and bishop feared the outcome of the congregation in the event of her death—no one else possessed the capabilities to lead them.

Mother Theodore received the sacrament known at that time as Extreme Unction. Now known as the Anointing of the Sick, the sacrament is administered more often to those in need of spiritual, emotional or physical healing. However, at that time, priests gave the sacrament only at the point of death, an indication of the seriousness of Mother Theodore's condition. With doctor's care and fervent prayer from the community, she gradually regained her strength.

Ill health continued for all the sisters during their first few years in America. Bitter cold winters contrasted with extremely hot summers. Their bodies were unaccustomed to such drastic fluctuations in temperature. In addition, the humidity in the summers felt suffocating and created a prime environment for disease-carrying mosquitoes. These mosquitoes caused one illness called Wabash ague, a form of malaria. Symptoms included chills and fevers; the disease remained in one's system indefinitely.

Mother Theodore's health had been compromised before coming to America and she never fully recovered. Along with her chronic digestive disorder, she also contracted several episodes of ague, "brain fever," pleurisy, and pneumonia. Illnesses came and went; each lasted several weeks at a time, with fewer and fewer healthy days in between.

In 1843, only three years after she first arrived in America, Mother Theodore returned to France on a mission to seek funding. Several situations at Saint Mary-of-the-Woods caused her tremendous stress. The strain of her many burdens and the arduous voyage took its toll on her health. After landing in New Orleans on her return home, she suffered from nausea and other stomach and intestinal ailments, fevers, and lung problems. She was so ill that the Ursuline Sisters located in that city cared for her for seven weeks.

Mother Theodore's illnesses increased with time in severity

and duration. Sickness often overcame her. Her weakened condition left her quite fragile. In 1850 while traveling on what she called "a crowded mud wagon" for twenty-four hours, she said she arrived at her destination "half dead." Her nose bled the entire ride.

Illness after illness prevented Mother Theodore from attending important events. Yearly retreats sustained the sisters spiritually and emotionally, and Mother Theodore longed to be with the sisters. More and more often, however, sickness prohibited her from joining the community for those retreats. She also missed the consecration of Bishop Bazin.

Mother Theodore accepted ill health as a part of her path to heaven. She believed that God had a reason for sending or, at the very least, permitting illness. She said it assisted in her sanctification. Perhaps this made Mother Theodore more conscious of her need to prepare for death; she advised her sisters to do the same, to be ready for the day the Lord called them home.

In addition to the spread of many other diseases, cholera outbreaks were common. Often the sisters cared for the sick during an epidemic, putting themselves at great risk of contracting the illness themselves. Mother Theodore told her sisters to ensure that nothing rested heavy on their souls, particularly during those periods of uncertainty.

In March of 1849, Mother Theodore wrote to the sisters at Madison. She advised them to be cheerful and kind to one another. She told them to prepare for the summons of the Divine Savior. She added matter-of-factly, "If you have to die, well my daughters, die for Him who died for you."

Placing Everything in God's Hands

Especially in the midst of very challenging situations, relinquishing all control to Providence is not easy for most of us. Placing our problems in God's hands and letting go takes practice and restraint. Typically we say that we believe God will answer our prayers, but then we take that problem back by trying to fix it ourselves. We continue to worry and fuss over it.

We live very differently than Mother Theodore, but she knew pain, sorrow, hardships and loss as well as anyone. In spite of it all, she trusted in God's love and concern for humanity with every ounce of her being. Mother Theodore showed us that if we trust in the Lord with all of our hearts and give glory to God in all that we do, God will protect us and show us our path to heaven.

THREE WAYS TO FOLLOW
SAINT MOTHER THEODORE BY

TRUSTING IN PROVIDENCE

1. Pray before the tabernacle or Blessed Sacrament one day each week.

2. Visualize holding one of your problems in your hands and offering it to God. Repeat this visualization each time that particular worry comes to mind. Observe what happens to the problem over time.

3. Before going to sleep at night, recognize three blessings in your life and give thanks to God for each of them.

*And he said to them, "Go into all the world
and proclaim the good news to the whole creation."*
                                          —*Mark 16:15*

Principle #3
Spread the Word

Mother Theodore grew up at the end of the French Revolution, a pivotal point in French history. One regime after the other took over the ruling government in France. Republicanism finally replaced the absolute monarchy, but the political environment remained unstable for decades.

Prior to the French Revolution of 1789–1799, the privileged nobility class governed France. King Louis XVI and his queen, Marie Antoinette, lived an opulent lifestyle that contributed significantly to the country's deficit. In the meantime, the government heavily taxed commoners to support the upper classes and the country's support of the American Revolution. Unemployment and food shortages created mounting resentment.

In addition to the turmoil in government, the intolerance of the Church in France angered the oppressed. They reacted with a violent sweeping out of the clergy, hierarchy and religious sisters. Many found themselves imprisoned or put to death. Others fled the country or lived in seclusion. Tensions subsided with the agreement between Napoleon and Pope Pius VII, called the Concordat of 1801. The new government forced the Church to relinquish its property, but in time, did allow the bishops, priests and sisters to return with some restrictions. Slowly the Church in France began to recover.

In the town of Ruillé-sur-Loir, the Reverend Jacques Fran-cois Dujarié emerged from hiding to set up a school with the as-sistance of two young women. He realized that the future of the country rested on the children. Much work needed to be done for an uneducated generation with little to no religious foundation. Father Dujarié recruited other women to join them. Within a few years the group rapidly increased in number and evolved into the Sisters of Providence.

The first house in which the women lived, fondly referred to as "Petite Providence," was very small. Father Dujarié personally gathered the stones to build it. As the group grew, a larger home replaced the little structure. The order's most famous member, Sister Theodore Guérin, entered the religious life in that house.

Evangelizing France

Mother Theodore realized the need for religious women in her country and joined the young congregation of the Sisters of Providence in 1823. Novices received little training due to the immense and immediate need for them. Soon after professing her first vows, the mother superior sent Mother Theodore to work in the town of Preuilly-sur-Claise.

In 1826, Mother Theodore received a transfer to the Saint Aubin parish in Rennes and was appointed superior. This was a daunting assignment for someone with so little experience as a religious. However, during her eight years there, Mother Theodore transformed the character of an entire town.

Rennes topped the list of the most challenging areas of France in which to work. Mother Theodore cared for more than 600 very difficult pupils there. The immoral and inattentive community produced unruly children. Parents unconcerned with their children's education and religious growth gave Mother Theodore no support.

Mother Theodore entered the chaotic environment with a calm, sweet reserve. She truly loved and respected the students. In contrast to previous teachers, recognized as strict disciplinarians, Mother Theodore inspired and encouraged. She rewarded good behavior.

At first the children did not know how to react to her. No one ever treated them with such tenderness and patience. Gradually they began taking a new interest in their studies and their own academic excellence. The change in the students transferred to their families. Within months the town's personality improved — one child, one family at a time. When Mother Theodore was transferred from Rennes, she left behind a vibrant community of faith that had grown attached to their beloved leader.

Within a short period of time at the new parish, the people there became fond of Mother Theodore and began to develop under her direction. She even convinced an aristocrat in the area, Monsieur de la Bertaudière, to build a village church. In gratitude for her six years of service in Soulaines, parishioners wrote Mother Theodore's name in memorial notes and buried them in the cornerstone of the building.

She also grew personally during her time in Soulaines. She appreciated the smaller, gentler parish. Due to her lightened workload, she found time to study under a local doctor, gaining medical knowledge that proved invaluable to her in the future. The reduced level of responsibility also benefited her health.

Evangelizing America

In 1839, on the request of Bishop Simon Bruté of Vincennes, Indiana, in the United States, the Very Reverend Celestine de la Hailandière returned to his homeland of France to recruit missionaries. While there, Bishop Bruté passed away. Father de la Hailandière became his successor.

The new bishop of Vincennes approached Mother Mary Lecor of the Sisters of Providence to request her assistance. Mother Mary agreed to help, but with some conditions. She said she could not spare many sisters, and she refused to assign anyone to the mission. Sisters had to volunteer.

When Mother Mary offered the missionary opportunity to the community, Mother Theodore did not submit her name for consideration. She thought herself of little value because of her fragile health. On the contrary, Mother Mary said she didn't command Mother Theodore to go, but insisted that no sister leave for America if Mother Theodore did not agree to lead them. Mother Mary wrote previously to the bishop, "We have only one Sister capable of making the foundation. If she consents, we shall send you Sisters next summer." That capable sister was Mother Theodore.

The New World greatly needed teachers and religious leaders. Immigrants flooded into America in incredible numbers. A million and a half newcomers immigrated during the 1840s, and over two and a half million did so in the 1850s. The opportunity for religious and economic freedom prompted the influx. People fled to the United States in pursuit of their own dreams. With the growth of manufacturing, both the Old and the New World experienced difficulty with economic independence, but America offered far better opportunities than Europe.

Immigrants at that time came predominantly from Scandinavia, Germany, Great Britain and Ireland. This created a proud and diverse pool of people of various nationalities and faiths. Catholics mixed with Protestants and tried to live together for the most part, although a strong strain of anti-Catholicism ran through America.

The political parties fluctuated between the Democrats and Whigs, which eventually gave way to the Republicans. Seven presidents served during Mother Theodore's sixteen years in the United States. Martin Van Buren served the end of his term as president when she arrived in 1840. William Harrison, John Tyler, James Polk, Zachary Taylor, Millard Fillmore and Franklin Pierce followed. The United States of America was a country in physical transition as well, rapidly expanding in land acquisitions. The Union was comprised of twenty-six states when Mother Theodore arrived; five more joined by the time of her death in 1856.

Mother Theodore headed for the state of Indiana, which entered the union in 1816. Once a territory occupied by Native Americans of the Delaware, Shawnee, Miami and Pottawatomie tribes, by the early 1800s the French, French Canadians and Germans had predominately settled there. Of an estimated 250,000 children in Indiana, less than 50,000 enrolled in school. Those who did attend were educated either in public schools funded by tuition or small private schools. It wasn't until the 1850s that taxes supported schools in most northern states.

The area greatly demanded teachers, in particular, teachers who could teach Catholic doctrine and values along with academics, music and art. Mother Theodore recognized her responsibility to answer the call to spread the gospel in the New World as she did in her own country. She was forty-one years old and suffering from unstable health when she left the motherhouse in Ruillé, France, on July 12, 1840. Five young, religious women accompanied her: Sister Saint Vincent Ferrer Gagé, Sister Basilide Sénéchal, Sister Olympiade Boyer, Sister Mary Xavier Lerée, and Sister Mary Liguori Tiercin. The women had little knowledge of what they were about to encounter on their voyage to and then across America. They only knew of the need to teach and spread the Word of God.

No Earthly Attachments

When Jesus sent his disciples out to proclaim the kingdom of God, he told them to leave everything behind. He wanted them to concentrate on their mission without the distraction of earthly goods or loved ones. Missionaries take those instructions to heart even today.

The American mission required a great sacrifice of the sisters—to leave family, friends and homeland with the understanding they may never return. Mother Theodore wrote in her journal that it felt as if she and the sisters accompanying her were being exiled from France. They did not speak when they left the motherhouse. Amid many muffled sobs, Mother Theodore advised the sisters to offer their heavy hearts to God.

She also told them not to be concerned for themselves and their sorrow over what or who they left behind. They did not

belong to anyone or any place on earth. They only belonged to
God. She said, "The true country of a Christian, but above all of
a Religious, is Heaven, towards which we are tending; it is for
God that we have made this sacrifice, and I may add, He has
already repaid us, for His protecting hand has assisted us in a
visible manner, and we cannot but recognize the attentions of
His Providence."

Years later, in a letter to postulants from Belgium headed
from France to the United States, Mother Theodore wrote that
the Lord called them to be not only faithful spouses of Christ but
true apostles, leaving all that is dear to them. The acceptance of
the mission required a solid foundation. "One cannot belong to
God in an imperfect manner and be happy here," she said. "If
your heart wavers, if you are afraid of the cross, of poverty, of hu-
miliations, do not leave France; you would not be suitable for our
little Community. If on the contrary you are determined to belong
entirely to God, to endeavor by His grace to become humble, pious, and above all, to renounce your own will by obedience, then
come. Our Blessed Lord will assist you and protect you. He will
be your guide in your long and hazardous voyage." She added
that the sisters at Saint Mary-of-the-Woods loved them already
and prayed for them.

In the United States, the sisters witnessed a level of poverty
not seen before. The first priests Mother Theodore encountered
in the Midwest were so poor that she thought no one believed
her description when she wrote to her friends in France. Nothing equaled the poverty of the cathedral and clergy of the Vincennes Diocese, the diocese in which they planned to reside.
They found churches in ruins with broken windows and crum-

bling chimneys. The rectories consisted of dilapidated cabins with little furniture or protection from the elements. Priests slept on the cold floor or rough, hard benches. Mother Theodore said that the priests looked more like beggars than clergy. They wore tattered shoes and clothes with frayed collars. Their meager diets consisted only of cornbread.

However, the demeanor of the priests amazed Mother Theodore most of all. The priests appeared happy. Their work gave them so much joy that peace surrounded them. She said that scattering the good seed of the Holy Word upon the soil of the new land filled them with contentment.

Upon arriving in Indiana, Mother Theodore learned that the church once there burned to the ground the previous February. Bishop Bruté purchased that plot of land in 1838 from the Thralls family for fifteen dollars. Just less than two acres, the bishop named it Sainte Marie des Bois, Saint Mary-of-the-Woods.

The tiny remaining rectory served as both church and home for the parish priest. The altar stood opposite the priest's bed, table, chair and desk. It consisted of three planks supported by two stakes. A small piece of cotton spread over the planks served as the altar cloth. There was no tabernacle.

The home in which the sisters lived was adjacent to that property and belonged to the Thralls. The family of eight welcomed Mother Theodore, her five companions, and the four American postulants waiting to join them, into their modest home of four rooms and a loft. They allotted the use of one room and a shed for the ten sisters. The Thralls stored corn in half of the loft; the sisters slept in the other half. After living together for five weeks, the Thralls graciously sold their farmhouse to Bishop de la Hailandière, and the family relocated to another home they owned. The sisters then used the entire farm house.

The friendship the sisters maintained with "Uncle Joe and Aunt Sallie," as they affectionately called Mr. and Mrs. Thralls, remained life-long. Thralls descendents continue to live in and near Saint Mary-of-the-Woods and fondly recount their family connection to Mother Theodore.

The community's financial situation remained strained on and off for many years. At one point Mother Theodore only had one dollar on which to run the motherhouse and the schools they established throughout Indiana and Illinois. That dollar didn't even belong to her. A friend loaned it to her.

Food was sometimes scarce during those first years in the Indiana forest. Like the priests, the sisters' diet consisted of corn-bread and little else. When their chaplain, Father John Corbe, caught a squirrel, they made squirrel soup or stew. Occasionally sisters at some of the missions ate nothing for days. However, their situation did improve gradually over the next few years, because they grew fruits and vegetables in their garden according to the season. They raised some chickens, pigs and dairy cows for milk and butter.

The sisters also needed to acclimate to the fluctuating Indiana weather conditions. In addition to the hot, humid summers and bitter-cold winters, storms, lightning and roaring winds terrified them. The thousands of fireflies, swarms of mosquitoes, the howling of "wild beasts," and snakes that intruded into the classrooms gave them daily concerns.

Perhaps the most disheartening of all sacrifices the sisters endured was the loneliness. Since leaving behind their families in France, they grew close to one another. But even contact between the sisters was limited. They scattered across the missions established throughout Indiana and Illinois. The separation from one another deeply saddened them.

Mother Theodore said she understood their sadness, but advised them not to complain. "We cannot do our work if we all stay in the nest," she said. The work needed to be done, and the sacrifices made should be offered to God. She later told her friend, Father Chasse, that they would lay down their lives for the souls that must be won for God.

Endless Opportunities to Spread the Word

Mother Theodore never missed an opportunity to introduce the love of God. On a voyage back to France in 1843, she enjoyed praying the rosary with the Creoles on board. She also engaged in many pastoral opportunities with a rather rough group of people residing in the lower deck of the ship. Mother Theodore treated them kindly and respectfully. Although her gentleness was part of her natural demeanor, she knew that God's love must radiate through her actions as well as her words. The passengers returned the respect. They depended upon Mother Theodore to tend to their sick and even baptize an infant. She said she felt a deep sense of gratitude for the opportunity to serve them.

In America the sisters found many people who did not know God. In addition, many baptized Christian children knew little of their faith. Mother Theodore told her sisters that they needed to make up for the negligence of the parents with zeal and fervor. Sometimes the amount of work to be done appeared overwhelming. Mother Theodore advised, "Let us do what depends on us to advance the glory of our dear Jesus, the Spouse of our souls and of His Holy Church. After that, let us remain in peace; for we are not called upon to do all the good possible, but only that which we can do."

Not only did the sisters promote the faith to unbelievers, they also faced people with great religious prejudices. Only a few years before their arrival in the United States, riots took place on the East coast. In this country where people came to practice their religion freely, some did not want that freedom extended to Catholics.

When the sisters arrived in New York their first acquaintances recommended that they wear secular clothing until they reached their destination in Indiana. When they did wear their habits, on a steamboat down the Ohio River, a group of women with whom they shared their living quarters laughed at and teased them. The sisters' inability to speak English put them at an even greater disadvantage.

Persecution continued for many years throughout America. Bigots desecrated and burned churches and religious institutions. The most violent riots occurred in Philadelphia in May of 1844. Even private Catholic homes risked destruction in some areas, particularly on the East Coast. A Protestant opposition group called the Know-Nothings geared up to fight any advancement of Catholics and other immigrants.

A mayor in one of the towns where the sisters taught tried to persuade the sisters to use school books that the town provided. Those books did not contain any religious reference. Mother Theodore forbid the sisters to accept such offers, even though it would save them a considerable amount of money. In a letter to

Sister Basilide on June 9, 1852, she wrote, "Let those people keep their money and let us alone. I would rather throw the money into the river than expose the faith of our children. They do not want the Blessed Virgin, nor pictures of the Saints—those good people could even do without God! Such villains! They put me in bad humor."

Later when dealing with prejudice in the little towns surrounding Saint Mary-of-the-Woods, Mother Theodore warned the sisters to think carefully about their words and actions so as not to fuel any animosity. "Carefully guard every word; watch over yourselves that nothing imprudent may escape you and thus give the ill-disposed a reason for their complaints."

You the Evangelist

The life of an evangelist, and especially a missionary, is one of sacrifice. Mother Theodore and her sisters put their emotional and physical welfare at risk to serve others. They left behind all that they knew and loved for a life that included hunger and poverty. They encountered multiple illnesses, many that caused lifelong complications. Some of the sisters died from those diseases.

Mother Theodore did not complain about what they lost or what never was to be. Her only concern was to bring the gospel to people who did not know God and help maintain the faith in those who did. She prompted spiritual growth in her students and the Sisters of Providence. She spread the teachings of Jesus in her spoken and written words. She also illustrated these teachings by her daily actions. We are all called to do the same.

Mother Theodore asked, "What comfort is there for those

who do not pray?" We ask the same question, because we know that we gain strength from prayer and the knowledge that we are not alone. As Mother Theodore so beautifully said, "In the midst of a storm, how sweet is the calm the soul finds in the Heart of Jesus." We have hope in knowing that God hears our prayers. God is with us at all times and listens to our cries for help.

We answer Mother Theodore's question by introducing prayer to people who have not had the opportunity to know of God's love. We are obligated as Christians to teach the Scriptures and what can be learned from the holy books, especially the gospels. We are to do our part as evangelists to spread the message of the coming of the kingdom of God in our hometown, in our country, and across the globe.

Being evangelists will present us with many challenges, but Jesus promised that we will be richly rewarded if we follow him. "Jesus said, 'Truly I tell you, there is no one who has left house or brothers or sisters or mother or father or children or fields, for my sake and for the sake of the good news, who will not receive a hundredfold now in this age—houses, brothers and sisters, mothers and children, and fields, with persecutions—and in the age to come eternal life'" (Mark 10:29-30).

THREE WAYS TO FOLLOW
SAINT MOTHER THEODORE AND

SPREAD THE WORD

1. Read the Bible daily. Find a book on the Bible that is
    written at your level and read it. Participate in a Bible
    study group at your church.

2. Learn about the work of missionaries around the world.
    Imagine yourself as a missionary in a foreign land. Now
    imagine yourself as a missionary to those around you in
    your daily life.

3. Practice being an evangelist without words. Allow your
    actions to speak for your beliefs in your workplace, at
    home, and in your community.

But it is not so among you; but whoever wishes to become great among you must be your servant, and whoever wishes to be first among you must be slave of all. For the Son of Man came not to be served but to serve, and to give his life as a ransom for many.

—Mark 10:43-45

Principle #4
Lead by Serving

Mother Theodore was a superb leader. She visualized the possible outcomes of every option. She clearly understood her potential, limitations, and the actions necessary for the best future results of the community and missions. She knew when to take action, when to submit to superiors, and when to share responsibility.

Mother Theodore possessed great courage, a strong sense of vision, and keen instinct. She excelled in her communication and listening skills. She remained energetic in spite of her chronic weakened health condition and functioned effectively under tremendous stress. She thought independently and understood how to work within a hierarchy.

Leadership qualities were evident in Mother Theodore as early as the age of fifteen when she took over the care and support of her family. She served them by accepting full responsibility for their care and that of their home. No longer did she simply perform as "sister" to her sibling, Marie-Jeanne. She became nurse, breadwinner, teacher, spiritual counselor, and a maternal figure as well.

The ability and courage to think and act independently continued to be visible once Mother Theodore entered the religious life. Whatever position she chose or to which her superiors appointed her, she wholeheartedly invested her time, talent and wisdom. In France, she wasn't merely a teacher but rather an award-winning educator. She didn't just work in a ministry but developed into an inspiration for an incredible legacy that continues today in the community of the Sisters of Providence of Saint Mary-of-the-Woods and Saint Mary-of-the-Woods College in Indiana.

Mother Theodore was proactive. She knew her capabilities and didn't hesitate to take control of a situation. On her transatlantic voyage in 1843, the captain of the ship became ill after an altercation with a drunken sailor. Mother Theodore quickly approached the captain. She feared that he suffered from "congestion of the brain" and prepared to "bleed him," a common medical remedy of the time. She felt relieved when he responded immediately after she began the invasive intervention. Anyone else might have hesitated to interfere: The responsibilities and consequences resulting from such an action were a great a risk. But Mother Theodore realized it was imperative to assist the captain because of the need for his leadership. Only the captain was qualified to direct the long ocean journey ahead in the most volatile season.

Mother Theodore held a realistic sense of business. She recognized what tools the sisters needed to attain success at their missions. She tailored the education and training for each assignment appropriately. For example, she realized the necessity for her French teachers to master the English language. In spite of the significant call for the Sisters of Providence to open schools throughout Indiana, that need required balance with adequate preparation. Sending out the sisters too soon minimized their ability to succeed. It was imperative that they arrived at their establishments capable of teaching in the English language. For that reason, she held the French Sisters at the motherhouse at least a year longer than the American-born sisters.

Mother Theodore's leadership style reflected how Jesus led his disciples. Jesus did not retain complete control of evangelizing the world. Scripture tells us that he sent his disciples out to preach and heal. He made every follower accountable for carrying on the ministry. In the same way Mother Theodore realized the amount of work needed to be done in the New World. However, she did not expect to accomplish everything herself. The success of the American mission did not rest solely on her shoulders. All current and future Sisters of Providence of Saint Mary-of-the-Woods shared in that responsibility.

From the very beginning she divided the workload at the motherhouse carefully. Mother Theodore assigned sisters to positions according to their capabilities, whether it included tailoring, cooking, caring for the sick, teaching, or tending to the fields. Maintaining the welfare of the community depended upon the achievement of every position.

Mother Theodore also recognized the necessary division of leadership for the foundation's success in carrying on in the event of Mother Theodore's incapacitation or death. When she found her sisters to be sufficiently trained, she advised the community to elect a First Assistant and Mistress of Novices from the group. In addition to preparing the community for her absence, this administrative decision relieved some of the weight of the responsibility from Mother Theodore's shoulders.

Serving Others as She Led

First and foremost, Mother Theodore was a religious woman. In her humble way she sought to follow God's will rather than her own. As a servant leader, she rolled up her sleeves and physically participated in her missions. She taught in the classroom, cared for the field animals, tended the crops in the garden, coordinated building construction with the workers, and tucked herself away in her office with stacks of paperwork.

Mother Theodore practiced what business writer Steven Covey calls "Principle-Centered Leadership." Besides the typical leadership traits, the people around Mother Theodore knew her to be reliable, service-oriented, and proactive. She was concerned for the people involved. She sought to understand rather than become frustrated or angry at those who did not understand her or her mission.

Christ reigned prominently at the heart of Mother Theodore's thoughts, words and actions, and therefore also at the heart of her guidance. Compassion, justice, forgiveness and service guided her when she prepared, supported and offered advice to the sisters, employees and students. Her leadership abilities always aimed for the greater good.

The Sisters of Providence of Saint Mary-of-the-Woods began as a community of two cultures that needed to carefully blend together into an effective team. Mother Theodore's concern focused on how she best served and insured the well-being of the French- and American-born sisters. She appreciated and honored the cultural differences of both.

At one time, the community considered returning to France because of difficulties with the local Indiana bishop. Mother

Theodore knew the challenges such a move presented to the American-born sisters and sought every viable solution to avoid the dilemma of either transporting the Americans to France or leaving them behind in the United States. Fortunately, because of Mother Theodore's skill at reaching compromises, the decision never needed to be made.

Effective and Firm

Mother Theodore respected authority. As the superior general, she also knew that the entire community of the Sisters of Providence of Saint Mary-of-the-Woods depended on her to defend their identity and lead them successfully in their missions. For this reason, she demanded the women's rights and preserved the order's purpose and intentions.

One such incident that required these leadership skills occurred between the Sisters of Providence and Father Kundek at the Jasper mission. Father's agreement with the sisters required teachers sent there to be fluent in both German and English. The school planned to be open to children whether or not they were capable of paying tuition. Students included girls of any age and boys up to thirteen, except for any aged student in need of religious instruction in preparation of First Holy Communion. In exchange for all this, Father promised the sisters the use of a house, one hundred dollars a year, flour, meat, sugar and coffee, and access to the sacraments and daily Mass.

When Father did not give the sisters their due, Mother Theodore insisted on nothing less than promised. She remained calm and kind in her dealings with Father Kundek but adamantly insisted on the terms being honored in full. She reminded him that the future of the establishment remained in his hands. She approached him compassionately but as an effective business-person.

More importantly Mother Theodore refused to submit to conditions contrary to the rules of her organization. When Bishop de la Hailandière of the Vincennes Diocese admitted postulants—candidates interested in joining the order—and installed them in missions of his choosing without Mother Theodore's consent, she intervened. She knew the qualities necessary for success in her community and reserved her right to make such determinations. She also fought for the order's independence to perform its ministries in the way it intended from its inception.

For example, Mother Theodore repeatedly demanded that the bishop turn over the deed to the property of Saint Mary-of-the-Woods to the community. The original agreement made between the bishop and her superior, Mother Mary Lecor in France, stated this. The bishop's refusal to meet these terms deterred the sisters from expanding the facilities. Mother Theodore knew it was not prudent to continue building on property they did not own, yet they desperately needed to do so. She told the bishop to give the deed to the Sisters of Providence or they would relocate to another diocese.

The ongoing arguments between Mother Theodore and the bishop resulted in great animosity on his part. He commanded her to write a letter of apology. Mother Theodore sent a letter stating that she apologized if she overstepped the rules of politeness, and perhaps even the respect due to him, but she refused to yield to his demands. She stood firm and held her ground, with full knowledge of the probable repercussions.

Mother Theodore also affirmed her rights with the local government. In 1844, the authorities accused her of passing counterfeit money. She defended herself effectively. However, she said it disheartened her that any official in her adopted country thought her capable of committing such a crime.

What's more, she fought for the order's right to remain tax-free. The government did not require the religious community to pay taxes but pressured them to do so. She also had the foresight to incorporate the congregation in January of 1846, after the French sisters became naturalized citizens. Their new status significantly improved their business possibilities and financial situation.

Throughout those dealings, public officials found Mother Theodore to be a formidable opponent. A woman, much less a religious woman, didn't customarily take such assertive stances.

Mentor and Role Model for Christian Leadership

A mentor is a special kind of leader. She is a role model, instructor, sounding board, guide, and advisor. She shares her experiences, talents, knowledge, wisdom, and key contacts with a most fortunate protégé—the recipient of this powerful gift.

A mentor supports a protégé's growth at the protégé's own pace and in her own way. She identifies talents of which the protégé may not be aware. A mentor builds a launching pad from which her protégé can fly and a safety net in the event she falls. She provides opportunities to grow and significant people with whom to network.

We often think of mentoring in the business world, but there are many other forms. Mentoring is tremendously empowering and allows a quicker and more efficient avenue to success in any area of life. Not only can it jumpstart a career, it can promote a higher level of parenting, spirituality, financial capability, relationship building, and critical thinking.

Mother Theodore was the epitome of a mentor. She masterfully instructed and counseled the young women under her supervision. She encouraged and supported her protégés. She also loved the women in her care like daughters. She realized that the Sisters of Providence of Saint Mary-of-the-Woods embarked on a journey of vital importance. The women left their families and friends to evangelize, educate and care for the children of the frontier. And if the sisters were to be successful in their mission, Mother Theodore needed to be successful in hers.

The ripple of Mother Theodore's mentoring had limitless potential. Every sister she elevated, elevated the children around her, and those children in turn possessed the possibility of elevating the people around them. The trail of progress might very well continue without end. In fact, it does—as anyone who knows the history of the Sisters of Providence of Saint Mary-of-the-Woods can attest.

Mother Theodore believed mentoring in the classroom to be particularly important because it touched the segment of society that determined the future of the world. A teacher can disseminate information simply by standing in front of a class and spouting off facts and concepts. In contrast, a mentoring teacher inspires students to investigate further on their own. She excites the students with the fascinating workings of a magnificent planet. She encourages them and reveals the expansive reach within each student's own grasp.

Staff and students recognized Mother Theodore as a mentoring teacher at parishes in France and also in the United States. Mother Theodore insisted that her sisters teach in the same way as she did. She held the students' well-being, happiness, and desire to learn as priorities. As important as the studies were, Mother Theodore also stressed to her sisters that the students learned by example. She insisted that her teachers be exemplary role models.

She often told them that as good religious women, they must focus on how they affected the children and adults around them, not the other way around. Mother Theodore showed how to do this by her words and actions. She carefully chose her words and how she said them. She spoke and acted gently, thoughtfully and affectionately.

Balanced Guidance

Mother Theodore said that the sisters must accept challenges as part of earthly life. She showed them how to do this from the time she claimed Indiana as her home, leaving all she loved across the sea. She once wrote that "the cross" awaited them at every turn. As long as they lived on this earth, there would be pain. It paved the way to heaven.

Once she sent the sisters to schools they established throughout the area, personal contact between them was limited to yearly visits, when Mother Theodore saw her sisters at their missions, and retreats back at the motherhouse, when as many of the sisters as possible convened. As a result, much of Mother Theodore's professional mentoring with the sisters occurred through writing. She wrote prolifically. It is estimated that Mother Theodore wrote nearly five thousand lengthy, informative letters addressed to numerous friends, peers and protégés.

Mother Theodore often apologized for her handwriting. She once said, "My letters are so poor that I dare not read them over after they are written." She probably struggled to write to the extent she did, since she often didn't feel well. She never would have guessed how often her letters would be read over and over again, year after year, by countless people worldwide. In addition to being sometimes quite poetic, it is remarkable how sensible and timeless her letters are. She wrote them with the intention of being read by one specific person in a given period of time in history. But in those letters we continue to find solid guidance on how we too can live a holy life—in any age, at any age.

Mother Theodore carefully guided her protégés in a positive direction. She always used constructive words. Even in the event of a serious offense, she clearly defined the infraction, explained why she found it wrong, and offered alternatives. For example, Sister Basilide, one of the sisters who came to America from France with Mother Theodore, made several poor administrative decisions that created difficulty for Mother Theodore. With each instance, Mother Theodore explained why she deemed Sister Basilide's decision inappropriate. She did not dwell on the point. Once she discussed the incident, she viewed it as over.

On one occasion Sister Basilide authorized the acceptance of public school books and the inspection of her classrooms by public officials. Mother Theodore spelled out, as she did previously, why those decisions were not acceptable. She said that the sister's actions distressed her mother superior. But with that, the discussion ended. She did not raise the topic again.

Mother Theodore gave the same advice to all the sisters in regard to recognizing their own failings. In a letter to Sister Maria on November 24, 1854, she told her to think no more about her faults and not to become discouraged. She said that once Sister Maria committed a fault, she should acknowledge it, make amends when possible, try not to repeat the error, and move on.

She instructed the superior of each mission to respond to the sisters under their management in the same manner. Guidance required that the leader of each mission must correct errors, but how they gave the criticism made a tremendous difference on how the sisters accepted it. Mother Theodore insisted that all sisters be handled gently, firmly and privately.

On the other hand, Mother Theodore also quickly gave praise. She often told the sisters how they pleased her, especially when they indicated personal growth. She appreciated and acknowledged when a sister took criticism to heart and worked to improve her actions. For example, Mother Theodore wrote in a letter to one sister how happy the sister made her when she received her superior's advice without getting upset. Mother Theodore said, "It is a great consolation for a superior to be able to speak frankly to those of whom she has charge."

Mother Theodore loved the sisters and told them so very often. Many of the women left their homes at a young age. They suddenly found themselves isolated from family and peers. She knew the importance of letting them know how much she cared about them and valued the work they did. Mother Theodore addressed her letters to the sisters affectionately. She wrote, "To my dear Sister," and "My dearly beloved daughter." She told the sisters that no one loved them more than she did and closed her letters with, "Your devoted and affectionate Sister St. Theodore." The sisters loved Mother Theodore as well.

Mother Theodore felt especially fond of Sister Mary James since their first meeting. Sister Mary James entered the community four months after her mother's death. Her father died in an accident shortly after her birth, and so Sister Mary James thought of Mother Theodore as "doubly her mother," and told her so on many occasions.

Like any mother, Mother Theodore felt great concern for the health and welfare of her sisters. She told them to dress warmly in the frigid winters and to remove wet clothing immediately. She especially worried about her sisters in areas of cholera epidemics. Understanding how infectious diseases are spread, she told them to keep themselves, the children, and their surroundings clean, get enough sleep, and write often. She desperately wanted to hear from them and know how everyone was doing.

Mother Theodore did not expect from the sisters, or from anyone else, what they could not give. She knew that the Holy Spirit blesses each person with different gifts. Not everyone is capable of attaining the same level of achievement in the same areas. She also told her sisters not to expect the same virtues and qualities from everyone with whom they worked.

As an insightful mentor, Mother Theodore possessed the distinct ability of being able to identify potential where others could not. When young Irma le Fer de la Motte entered the order in France, Mother Mary Lecor told her she would be good for nothing but to love God. Mother Mary also thought of her as too frail to go to the United States. But Irma, who became Sister Francis Xavier, did go to the United States upon the eager invitation of Mother Theodore.

Mother Theodore recognized Sister Francis' intelligence, piety and compassion. The sister soon became an important leader in the community. She taught Latin and drawing at the Academy and assisted Mother Theodore in the training of the postulants and novices. The community also chose her as second assistant to Mother Theodore in 1848.

Mother Theodore also identified the great potential in Sister Mary Cecilia Bailly. Sister Mary Cecilia was well-educated, affluent and devout. As a young novice she accompanied Mother Theodore on her trip to France in 1843. The community chose her as first assistant to Mother Theodore and then directress of the Academy. Upon the death of Sister Francis, Mother Theodore recalled Sister Mary Cecilia to the motherhouse. Not long after that, the community elected her superior general when Mother Theodore passed away.

Mother Theodore's Mentors

Effective leaders know that they also require guidance. Support and criticism needs to be given to them too. Mother Theodore had a wide spectrum from which to choose. She looked to the laity, women religious, and clergy for her own mentoring.

Several of Mother Theodore's friends lived in France, such as the Countess of Marescot and Madame le Fer de la Motte, the mother of Sister Francis. Mother Theodore shared a close confidence with France's Queen Marie Amélie as well. Queen Amélie was a former Italian princess and a holy and charitable woman. She extended her generosity to Mother Theodore and the Sisters of Providence on more than one occasion.

Mother Theodore also claimed many friends within the American laity, Mrs. Silvia Parmentier among them. The Parmentiers belonged to a distinguished New York family devoted to caring for priests and women religious upon their arrival in America. Mrs. Parmentier welcomed Mother Theodore and her companions like family when they disembarked from the ship, the *Cincinnati*, in 1840. This act of kindness resulted in a friendship that continued the rest of their lives. Mrs. Parmentier collected donations on the East coast for the Sisters of Providence; she purchased bolts of fabric and other items with those funds and sent them to the community. In turn, Mother Theodore often wrote to Mrs. Parmentier to inform her of their progress.

Mother Theodore also found peer mentors from her religious community. Sister Francis Xavier ranked as one of her closest friends. Mother Theodore thought Sister Francis to be the holiest person she knew. Her death devastated Mother Theodore. The loss of her dear friend and confidant hurt her at least as much, if not more, than any other event in her life.

In addition Mother Theodore found several powerful mentors within the clergy. Reverend Augustine Martin became a trusted friend and counselor after the first retreat he led for the sisters in December of 1840. Reverend Julian Delaune and Reverend Joseph Kundek offered their guidance also.

No one was more devoted to the Sisters of Providence than the Reverend John B. Corbe. Father Corbe served as their Ecclesiastical superior and chaplain from 1842 until his death in 1872. He vowed to stand behind the community wherever it established. If the sisters decided to relocate to another diocese during the disagreement with Bishop de la Hailandière, Father Corbe planned to go with them.

Father Corbe ministered to the sisters during the challenging times of poverty and tensions with the bishop. Some of the events which tried them the most exhausted their chaplain also, but he never gave up on them. Mother Theodore called him a dear friend and father to her and the community.

The two bishops of Vincennes that Mother Theodore came to know after Bishop de la Hailandière became trusted advisors as well. Bishop John Stephen Bazin and Bishop de Saint Palais offered help as needed. They did not interfere with the community's daily functions. The bishops made themselves available to Mother Theodore at her discretion.

Perhaps the most important mentor of all to Mother Theodore was the Most Reverend J. B. Bouvier, Bishop of Le Mans, France. Bishop Bouvier supported Mother Theodore without fail. He generously showered her with his compliments, wisdom and direction. He gave her solid counsel and defended her on several occasions when she went up against Bishop de la Hailandière. Bishop Bouvier also helped the community financially at least once. After the fire at Saint Mary-of-the-Woods in October, 1842, he sent 1,000 francs to the sisters, whom he called "Daughters so dear to me."

You, the Servant Leader

Mother Theodore's legacy is a chain of mentoring that continues today. She set a mentoring precedent in her motherhouse and in her schools. She inspired her sisters to be powerful leaders who developed future leaders.

We too who are touched by Mother Theodore are to be more

than good parents, siblings, spouses, teachers, professionals, partners, ministers and so on. As Scripture tells us, we are to be servant leaders and mentors.

We all lead in various degrees. The people who surround us in our homes, churches, communities, work and country depend on us for guidance, friendship and support. We serve one another by sharing what we know, our special talents, and our contacts with other people who can benefit from our tremendous package of blessings.

In doing so, we give value to our own God-given gifts. We glorify the Lord by sharing our light and elevating our neighbors'. In keeping with the message at the close of every Mass, we lead one another to a better place by going forth to love and serve the Lord and one another.

THREE WAYS TO FOLLOW
SAINT MOTHER THEODORE AND

LEAD BY SERVING

1. Find someone, probably younger than you, and start to mentor him or her. It doesn't have to be anything formal. In fact, the person might not even know what you are doing. Just begin to share your talent, knowledge and wisdom with your protégé in any way that is appropriate.

2. If you find yourself in a position of supervising others, including children, inform them when their decisions are poor, offer better alternatives, and then put the incident behind both of you.

3. Write someone you view as a role model or mentor in your life and thank them for their influence. If you cannot find his or her address, or if he or she is deceased, write the letter anyway in thanksgiving for their generosity and remember that person in your prayers.

Finally, beloved, whatever is true, whatever is honorable, whatever is just, whatever is pure, whatever is pleasing, whatever is commendable, if there is any excellence and if there is anything worthy of praise, think about these things. Keep on doing the things that you have learned and received and heard and seen in me, and the God of peace will be with you.

— *Philippians* 4:8-9

Principle #5
Be Just and Kind

When Mother Theodore arrived in the United States, she examined how best to apply her tried-and-true French teaching methods with those practiced in America. She observed the schools managed by other religious orders and evaluated their textbooks and educational requirements. Subsequently she developed a diverse curriculum for the students at Saint Mary-of-the-Woods Academy. Americans sought education in more areas than academics alone. The first classes offered at the Academy included English composition, philosophy, chemistry, botany, biology and French, in addition to art, music and embroidery.

Of course she knew the importance of the classes. But Mother Theodore also said that the two most important virtues of a teacher are justice and kindness. A teacher's first and foremost approach needs to be one of love. Mother Theodore treasured every student for their own unique qualities and wanted the students to know this. She tenderly cared for each one, including the most difficult, and recognized the child as a God-given blessing to the world.

Mother Theodore cautioned one of her teachers to attend to all of the children equally. She said, "Be very guarded, my daughter, in your words and actions, also in your affections. Be careful lest you show more affection for one pupil than for another; this would produce a bad effect among the children, since all wish to be loved by you."

Mother Theodore also applied this guideline to adults. She expected the students to be rewarded when they excelled, as she herself did as a teacher. She didn't want too much attention to be drawn to bad behavior. She told her teachers that if they respected the children, the children in turn would respect the teachers and themselves.

People gravitated to Mother Theodore and remained life-long friends with her as a result of her kindness and concern for people. Some of these friends helped her initially. She showed her appreciation by returning their generosity and friendship. The Brassier family offers a fine example.

Mother Theodore met Thomas Brassier and his family on the ship, the *Cincinnati*. She took him, his wife, and six children under her protection during the voyage, and they became close friends. Mother Theodore invited Thomas to work for the community. Months after the journey, she loaned him money to follow her to Saint Mary-of-the-Woods. Brassier descendents continued to live in the area for several generations.

Another longtime friend was Samuel Byerley, a wholesale grocer. Mother Theodore and the sisters met Samuel in New York in 1840. He carried the sisters' baggage from the custom house. Thereafter, he frequently sent sacks of coffee and barrels of sugar to them. Samuel later moved to the South Bend, Indiana, area to open a large dairy. When that business failed, Mother Theodore reciprocated his years of generosity by inviting him to send his two daughters to Saint Mary-of-the-Woods to be educated at the Academy without expense to him.

Serving the Poor and the Sick

Justice is a twofold condition. Everyone has both the right to justice and the responsibility to see that this same right is extended throughout society. We must provide others with what is entitled to us. The physically, mentally and financially healthy are obligated to provide for the poor, sick, hungry and underprivileged. Mother Theodore exemplified this dual obligation.

Mother Theodore's experience in caring for the sick began suddenly and without preparation at the age of fifteen years old when she looked after her own mother. That situation may be the force that drove her desire to study medicine and pharmacy under a doctor while serving in Soulaines, France. The training proved to be an invaluable investment of time for her American missionary work. Medical knowledge was rare on ocean voyages and in the vast unsettled territories of the North American continent. When Mother Theodore saw someone in need of medical attention, she happily cared for them. Her greatest concerns centered on the very young and the elderly on the ship. The crude accommodations and brutal storms at sea stressed them the most.

On several occasions Mother Theodore helped the passengers in the lower decks of the ship. She labeled the area "the antechamber of hell" because of the degree of fighting and foul language that spewed from there. However, to her surprise, she found that the atmosphere did quiet down with her presence. When she went down to them, they treated her with respect and appreciation.

She continued to serve the sick in the American wilderness. Mother Theodore and the Sisters of Providence tended to people requiring medical attention to the best of their ability. Although they were not physicians, their medical training proved adequate in assisting with common illnesses and injuries. In addition, the sisters opened free pharmacies for people who could not afford to purchase needed remedies.

Mother Theodore personally cared for sick students at the Academy. She kept notes on their illnesses in her journals. She also wrote to the children's parents to inform them of their progress.

Cholera was one of the most ravaging diseases of the time. The acute bacterial infection attacks the small intestine, producing symptoms of extreme diarrhea that depletes the body of fluids and salts. Victims decline rapidly. Mother Theodore knew of the outbreaks in New Orleans, St. Louis, Cincinnati and Louisville by the late 1840s. The disease typically spread in the summer heat under unsanitary conditions. Hundreds of people died each year.

Cholera hit humid areas particularly hard. Mother Theodore wrote of how the river overflowed in parts of New Orleans, leaving bodies to float in the waters and the air to become thick with stench. She blamed the plague on greedy people who insisted on traveling in and out of those towns for business and, consequently, spread the disease.

"But the Americans must have the 'dollar.' Their cupidity renders them daring and indifferent to everything else. It is nothing to them to expose their lives and those of others in order to gain money. How materialistic these people are! Not a single week passes that their indifference does not make our rivers the tombs of a great number of persons," she said.

Cholera attacked the village of Saint Mary-of-the-Woods and several surrounding cities in 1850. Sisters of Providence responded by caring for the sick. They also opened orphanages for children left behind by parents who succumbed to the disease. Mother Theodore loved all the children in her schools but especially sympathized with the orphans. Their sorrow touched her deeply. She told the sisters to be patient and treat them tenderly; as lovingly as their own children. The children needed a mother, and Mother Theodore encouraged her sisters to love and comfort them in that way.

She realized that compassion is at least as important as education. In a letter to Sister Mary Xavier, Mother Theodore warned against having a bad temper with the girls. She also said that the girls not only needed to learn how to sew but also how to be humble and patient by observing the example of the sisters.

Another growing health concern of the time was for people with mental disabilities. The general public barely understood this condition. Support for the mentally ill didn't result in special care at "mental asylums" until the late nineteenth century. Until then, families commonly committed their mentally disabled to prisons or hid them in their homes.

Mother Theodore cared deeply for these people, possibly because of her experience with her own mother. Once approached by a sister with a question on how to handle women with depression, Mother Theodore provided sound guidance. She then asked the sister to remember that when working with someone with depression or other mental conditions, the afflicted suffer more than they make the people around them suffer.

Oppression in America

America wrestled with a number of social issues when Mother Theodore arrived. In the land of the free, citizens adamantly demanded their independence in all ways of life. The Declaration of Independence clearly stated that all men are created equal and are entitled to a list of rights. Obviously, that document originally intended to guarantee total equality and freedom only for a segment of society—namely Caucasian, middle-to-upper-class males.

The mass majority held minorities of all races and creeds at a disadvantage. They offered women few rights. They looked upon Catholics with disdain. Many barred Irish immigrants from entrance to some businesses and rental apartments. They forced Native Americans from their fertile homelands to barren wastelands. Slave traders brought Africans and other people with dark skin from areas such as the Caribbean into this country against their will and sold them like heads of cattle.

Witnessing the appalling display of slave trading in Louisiana horrified Mother Theodore. She wrote to friends in France, "The most painful sight I saw in New Orleans was the selling of slaves. Every day in the streets at appointed places, negroes and negresses in holiday attire are exposed for this shameful traffic, like the meanest animals at our fairs. This spectacle oppressed my heart."

Mother Theodore knew that slavery contradicted all that America symbolized. She said, "These Americans, so proud of their liberty, thus make game of the liberty of others. Poor Negroes! I would have wished to buy them all that I might say to them, 'Go! Bless Providence. You are free!'"

Dutch traders brought the first Africans to Jamestown in

1619. Some of the earliest slaves received allowances to purchase their freedom after a given period of time, but that situation quickly changed. Escaping to states that did not allow slavery soon became the only means for most slaves to gain freedom.

Opposition to slavery rapidly mounted in the North by the 1800s, but the economy of the southern states depended on the slaves. Tobacco plantations reaped substantial profit with their free forced labor. The Northern states found this treatment of Africans to be morally offensive and demanded a change. Harriet Beecher Stowe's book, *Uncle Tom's Cabin*, published in 1852, helped to further expose the brutality of slavery to three hundred thousand readers in its first year of publication.

Tensions between the North and the South escalated for the next nine years, erupting into the Civil War in 1861. All slaves finally received their freedom in 1865, when Congress passed the Thirteenth Amendment to the Constitution that prohibited slavery in the United States. The law ended a practice of slave trading that continued in some areas on the North American continent for nearly 250 years and lasted 89 years after the founding of the United States of America.

Unfortunately, gaining freedom did not guarantee the fair or equal treatment of that person. Once free, even after the establishment of the Thirteenth Amendment, African and other Black Americans continued to be granted few rights. Both the North and South displayed this disparity.

Several other segments of society dealt with their own injustices as well. The influx of Catholic immigrants provoked concern from Protestants. The United States received massive immigration from Germany and Ireland. The Germans belonged to differing faiths, including Catholic, but nearly all of the Irish were devout Catholics.

Immigration from Ireland stemmed from suppression of the Irish by the British administration and rampant disease in their potato crop, their country's greatest food source. Nearly a million Irish people died during that famine. For many, emigration offered the only way to avoid starvation.

Most Irish immigrants arrived in this country destitute. They took any job for any pay. This condition allowed them to be exploited easily and resulted in job and housing discrimination. The Irish comprised more than half the labor force in the New England mills. Irish men were employed in the dirtiest and most dangerous positions. Irish women worked as servants, factory workers, seamstresses, and washerwomen. Even Irish children as young as four or five years of age labored in factories.

The Catholic Church was the heart of the Irish communities. It is there they found solidarity, emotional support, and spiritual nourishment. Many of these Irish immigrants, and German as well, settled in the Indiana and Illinois areas where the Sisters of Providence established missions to meet their needs.

Irish Catholic women found their situation to be compounded because of their gender, for society in general put women at a disadvantage. When Mother Theodore arrived in America the status of women ranked quite low. Any income a woman earned legally belonged to her husband. Women could not make wills or hold property in their own names without their husbands' approval. Those restrictions did not change until women gained the right to vote in 1920.

Women were restricted mostly to the role of homemakers—

maintaining the home and caring for the family. Only a handful of other professions opened to those fortunate enough to receive an advanced education. Those professions included nursing, teaching and library work.

No university allowed admission to women until 1833 when Oberlin College in Ohio allowed their entrance. In 1837, Wesleyan College in Georgia became the first all-women's college. The medical field became more of a professional possibility for women after Elizabeth Blackwell, the country's first female doctor, founded the Women's Medical College of Pennsylvania in 1850.

The many elementary schools Mother Theodore and the Sisters of Providence established in Indiana and Illinois offered excellent educational opportunities. Although the religious community desperately needed income, they accepted students who could not pay the tuition. The Catholic schools also accepted students belonging to other Christian denominations. Protestants made up approximately one third of their enrollment.

Mother Theodore believed the best way to solve the issues of poverty and inequality is through education. Education increases the realm of employment opportunities, thereby enhancing the ability to provide for one's family. Better employment positions lead to more lucrative jobs than the backbreaking, low-paying, manual labor ones otherwise available to the uneducated. This fact made the Academy at Saint Mary-of-the-Woods particularly important because when it opened its doors in 1840 no other school for higher education for women existed in Indiana.

In 1852, Mother Theodore wrote to her superior in France, "A woman in this country is only yet one-fourth of the family. I hope that, through the influence of religion and education, she will eventually become at least one half, the better half."

All God's Creatures

Mother Theodore said that if we love God, we will love, honor and respect God's creation. Her compassion extended to all of God's creatures. From the ants to the whales—with the possible exception of the swarms of hungry mosquitoes that invaded Saint Mary-of-the-Woods—the welfare of living things concerned her. She admired the beauty of all she encountered on land and sea.

Any small sign of affection from an animal won her over. One day after taking a long ride on her horse, Finette, Mother Theodore climbed down to find her habit covered in horse hair. Initially she became quite upset but her disposition quickly softened. "I believe I would willingly have given her to Mr. Crawford's mother, but the little rogue, guessing my thoughts, gave me so many caresses and showed herself so gentle that I was disarmed," she wrote to a friend.

A favorite pet at Saint Mary-of-the-Woods was a scrawny, yellow dog named Taillard. The sisters considered the dog a hero after it saved the convent from near destruction. Workers dumped coals into an ash barrel left against the frame building. When the smoldering coals launched into a full-blown fire, Taillard barked, alarming the sisters. They extinguished the fire before it caused any damage. Mother Theodore loved that dog and missed it terribly when it passed away late in 1853.

Mother Theodore found it painful to witness any animal harmed. On a ship back to America in 1843, a gale swept some chickens and a rabbit overboard. They vanished before anyone could save them. Mother Theodore sadly reflected on how only the day before she had put the little bunny in her pocket.

The conditions of farm animals on the prairie distressed her most of all. Farmers left the cows outdoors in all weather, the forest being their only shelter. It broke her heart to see them covered with rain, dew, and especially ice and snow. She said that in Vincennes the deafening cries of animals could be heard from morning till night. She also found it disturbing to see hogs' ears and tails mutilated and branded with identifying marks.

Your Responsibility to Seek Justice

Mother Theodore readily cared for the people around her. In France, on ocean voyages, and in America, she did her best to see that all people were treated equally and kindly. She shared her medical training, love, prayers, and her personal possessions with the sisters, students and people she met all along her life's path. She also worked to give young people, especially young women, the education and training necessary to better provide for themselves and their families.

Unrest develops in people who do not have access to the basic needs for survival, while justice and prayer leads to peace. If we want peace in the world, seeking the fair and compassionate treatment of all people is essential. In an address in early January, 2007, Pope Benedict XVI said, "The worsening scandal of hunger is unacceptable in a world which has the resources, the knowledge, and the means available to bring it to an end."

We cannot say that we do not know what is happening around the globe. We see the face of hunger every day on our televisions, the Internet, newspapers and magazines. Every city, no matter how affluent, has residents who lack sufficient food, clean water, housing or employment. Nor is it difficult to find people with mental and physical disabilities or children and elderly helplessly abandoned on the streets.

In our technologically advanced world of abundance, where money is available for extravagant luxuries, we have no excuse to over-consume and hoard. We can begin seeking justice with the people closest to us—members of our immediate and extended family, our church, and the community in which we live—and then outward into the world. Where there is more than needed, the excess, at the very least, should be sent to where there is not enough. We can make a difference even in a small way. For Scripture says:

> He has told you, O mortal, what
>   is good;
> and what does the Lord require of
>   you
> but to do justice, and to love
>   kindness,
> and to walk humbly with your God?
>   —Micah 6:8

It is not an option for us to meet the needs of our sisters and brothers. We are required to do so, so taught and exemplified by Mother Theodore.

THREE WAYS TO FOLLOW
SAINT MOTHER THEODORE AND

BE JUST AND KIND

1. Serve the hungry by donating canned goods and
    other nonperishable food items, toothpaste and other
    toiletries, and detergents to the nearest food pantry. You
    may also volunteer a few hours each week at a local
    shelter for homeless or battered women.

2. Learn how the rights of women and children could be
    improved and write letters to your local representative
    on their behalf. Look at issues such as equality in
    education, employment opportunities and wages.

3. Inform your friends that you do not wish to receive
    email with derogatory remarks or jokes against any
    segment of society, or hear such things spoken in your
    presence. And of course, never propagate any hurtful
    rumors about anyone.

Be on your guard! If another disciple sins, you must rebuke the offender, and if there is repentance, you must forgive. And if the same person sins against you seven times a day, and turns back to you seven times and says, 'I repent,' you must forgive.

—*Luke 17:3-4*

Principle #6
Forgive Like Jesus

C hristianity is founded on forgiveness. Through the great mercy of God, our sins are and continue to be forgiven. God became incarnate in the human form of Jesus and allowed himself to be tortured and killed for our salvation. Jesus forgave his persecutors with his last words. After everything that he endured he asked God to excuse the tormentors because they didn't understand what they did (Luke 23:34).

Throughout the scriptures we are told of the critical importance of forgiveness. Saint Paul told the Colossians that we have redemption and the forgiveness of sin in Jesus (Luke 1:13-14). He also told the Ephesians to be kind and forgiving to one another as God in Christ forgave them (Ephesians 4:32).

Mother Theodore often asked for forgiveness for the smallest of shortcomings. She began a letter to Father Joseph Kundek by asking his pardon for taking so long in responding to his prior letter. On February 14, 1842, she wrote that she was truly ashamed of herself.

After a minor misunderstanding between Mother Theodore and Father Martin, Mother Theodore wrote a letter of apology to the priest. She expressed her sorrow for giving him pain and explained what happened. She then added, "I do not say this by way of excusing myself. I see clearly that I did wrong and I ask your pardon."

Mother Theodore admitted her sins to God, herself and anyone she offended. She regularly participated in the sacrament of penance, now known as reconciliation. This sacrament provides the opportunity to examine one's conscience, admit any sins aloud, and receive absolution. Formerly, the sacrament focused on the recognition and admittance of our weaknesses and failings. Today the stress is on the opportunity to reconcile, to resolve and remove our differences with the Lord that we created by sinning. Sin is the turning away from God. When we sin, we choose to violate our relationship with God and create a separation between us. Mother Theodore received the Sacrament of Penance often so that nothing stood between her and God.

Respect for Authority

Several influential people created unwarranted suffering for Mother Theodore. However, she didn't dwell on the pain. She never spoke ill of the people who hurt her. She respected their position of authority and their point of view.

The first painful event resulted from a rumor. In the 1820s, Father Dujarié founded a congregation of brothers. He obtained loans for the brothers in the Sisters of Providence's name under his financial management. Mother Marie Madeleine du Roscoät, the first superior general of the Sisters of Providence of Ruillè, France, thought this to be the best decision at the time.

When Mother Marie Madeleine died suddenly in 1822, the community elected Mother Mary Lecor superior general. She requested that the two congregations be financially separated. When Father Dujarié did not comply, Mother Mary appealed to their bishop, who responded positively to Mother Mary's request in 1831.

Some time after that, while still in France, Mother Theodore stopped to visit Father Dujarié. She brought the priest some soup and sat with him for a while. One of the sisters reported the act of kindness to the current superior, Mother Saint Charles Jolle or Mother Mary. The two superiors considered Mother Theodore's gesture an act of opposition.

Unfortunately, they never discussed the matter with Mother Theodore. They didn't concern themselves with hearing her side of the event. Rather, Mother Saint Charles removed Mother Theodore from the large parish of Rennes after eight years of outstanding service and reassigned her to the small, less prestigious and distant community in Soulaines near Angers, France. She never gave an official explanation about the transfer to Mother Theodore.

On the insistence of her spiritual director, Bishop de Lesquen of Rennes, Mother Theodore sent an explanation to Mother Saint Charles of what really happened between her and Father Dujarié. Mother Theodore never received a response. She did not push to be understood. Instead she tried to see the situation from her superior's perspective, and ultimately she let it go.

Mother Theodore accepted her new position in Soulaines with humility and devotion to the new parish in which she served. Although disheartened over the disapproval of her superior, she soon found great happiness there. She studied nursing and basic medicine. She opened a free school and enjoyed teaching—especially mathematics—and the French government awarded her a medal of honor.

The community reelected Mother Mary Lecor in 1835 as superior general where she served until her retirement in 1871. Most likely, even during that brief period when she did not serve as superior general, Mother Mary influenced the management of the congregation. The sisters, including Mother Theodore, considered her to be a good superior. They admired, respected and loved her. However, the relationship between Mother Mary and Mother Theodore was complicated.

It appears that prior to Mother Theodore's departure from France, Mother Mary did care for her. Evidence also suggests that Mother Mary recognized Mother Theodore's potential. After all, she placed her in the most demanding positions, such as that of superior at the parish in Rennes. However, Mother Mary gave her somewhat backhanded compliments. In a farewell letter dated June 16, 1840, Mother Mary wrote to Mother Theodore, "God is my witness that I have ever loved you with a mother's heart, and that I shall always love you whether you be in Vincennes or in China—everywhere my love will follow you, even to heaven or to purgatory."

Many years later in the midst of very difficult times for Mother Theodore, Mother Mary wrote on January 29, 1847, "Consider, my dear Sister Theodore, that your case is a very uncommon one. You received the graces of the beginning; you speak the language of the country; you know the customs and the spirit. You were the one called to found that good work. It is from you it expects its life, increase and stability. I mean, of course, that you are the instrument of Providence, nothing more."

Mother Mary also criticized Mother Theodore. She offered little support or praise to her. She sent Mother Theodore to the untamed American frontier to found a congregation and schools without as much as a personal goodbye, adequate resources, sufficient personnel or any direction.

The state of communications at the time possibly prohibited faster replies, but Mother Mary rarely sent letters, the only means of sharing advice or friendship, with Mother Theodore. When a devastating fire at Saint Mary-of-the-Woods in 1842 left the American community in dire straits, Mother Mary didn't contact Mother Theodore for more than a year.

On one occasion the bishop of Le Mans advised Mother Theodore to accept a particular novice into her community at Saint Mary-of-the-Woods. Mother Mary told Mother Theodore to make her own decision. She didn't want to comment on the novice's suitability. When Mother Theodore did accept the novice, however, Mother Mary wrote of her disapproval. Mother Theodore responded in a humble way. She prayed for God to bless Mother Mary a hundredfold. She also asked her superior for forgiveness for "her faults."

Forgive and Forget

As with justice, forgiveness is twofold. When followers asked Jesus how to pray, he taught the prayer that we call the Our Father. Jesus said, "And forgive us our debts, as we also have forgiven our debtors" (Matthew 6:12). In this prayer we ask for our sins to be forgiven in the same way that we forgive.

Jesus also told the parable of the servant who did not forgive a fellow slave after the king forgave him. The king became so angry with the servant that he handed him over to be tortured and required him to repay his entire debt that he previously wiped out. Jesus said, "So my heavenly Father will also do to every one of you, if you do not forgive your brother or sister from your heart" (Matthew 18:35).

We are instructed to forgive as God forgives us. God waived the most serious of our offenses. We are to do the same. Jesus told Peter he must forgive someone who hurt him seventy-seven times. In other words, forgiveness is to be limitless (Matthew 18:21-22).

Mother Theodore's level of forgiveness is remarkable. When someone hurt her she tried to understand the situation from the other person's point of view. She used the opportunity to examine her own failings and quickly apologized and took responsibility for her actions (or lack thereof).

Father Stanislaus Buteux served as one of the earliest missionaries and the first chaplain at Saint Mary-of-the-Woods. He was a hardworking and intelligent man. He physically participated in building a convent for the sisters, as well as the first Academy building.

However, his goals for the community differed from that of the sisters. He intended to see the community run by Americans. He encouraged a young novice, Sister Aloysia, to position herself so that she replaced Mother Theodore. He persuaded the novice that she possessed the qualifications necessary and that this move could prove beneficial to the community. He expected Mother Theodore and her French sisters to assist her or settle elsewhere. Father Buteux attempted to influence the sisters to agree with him. He also tried to persuade Mother Theodore to resign, insisting that she lacked the qualifications to lead an American congregation.

The order recognized Sister Aloysia as a tremendous asset in transitioning the French sisters to the American ways at the beginning of her service. But as she gained more and more control of the daily affairs of the community, Mother Theodore and the sisters realized that Sister Aloysia's ambitions were to advance her own agenda and not that of the Sisters of Providence. Mother Theodore dismissed Sister Aloysia, leaving the order in a state of unrest. The woman later opened another school in Terre Haute to compete with the Sisters of Providence, and she spread lies about Mother Theodore, the sisters, and their capabilities as teachers.

Bishop de la Hailandière intervened in Father Buteux's attempts to undermine Mother Theodore. He replaced the chaplain with Father John B. Corbe. He also assured Mother Theodore of her qualifications. Sadly, the disharmony created among the sisters took many years to completely resolve.

Mother Theodore reacted by controlling the damage without anger or counter-negativity. She forgave her offenders and put the incident behind her. She restored peace in the community and affection between the sisters. She then encouraged the sisters to continue their usual practice of promoting academic excellence with skill and compassion. She asked them to concentrate on their responsibilities and not concern themselves with any opposition.

Pray for Offenders

The very same bishop who believed in her and brought her to America produced Mother Theodore's most difficult challenges. Bishop Celestine de la Hailandière's position was to be one of protector and advisor. Instead he crippled the advancement of

Mother Theodore and the Sisters of Providence in several ways. For example, he didn't allow them to utilize funds given to him for the specific use of the community. Nor did he turn over the deed to the property on which the motherhouse and school stood. Most of all, he held them under his control by refusing to approve the official Rule of the congregation.

The congregation was independent and self-governing. The sisters required a formal Rule defined by them and approved by their bishop in France and Bishop de la Hailandière. After the bishops approved the Rule, all decisions in regard to the order were to be made by the Sisters of Providence—with the guidance of the local bishop—but not by Bishop de la Hailandière.

Each religious congregation is governed by its own Rule. Today the Rule is the essence of their community. It defines their identity, guidelines and intentions by which they promise to live. It is similar to an organization's mission statement and bylaws, listing responsibilities and expectations of members and how funds and provisions are to be disbursed.

The lack of rules for the Sisters of Providence inhibited the selection of incoming sisters. Bishop de la Hailandière recruited and even inducted candidates into the order without Mother Theodore's approval. Most of his choices were unsuitable and later needed to be dismissed. He also assigned sisters to new missions. He did not equip the missions adequately or appropriately. The bishop even encouraged the sisters to vote Mother Theodore out of office on more than one occasion.

According to the proposed Rule, Mother Theodore visited all sisters stationed at the missions throughout Indiana and Illinois at least once a year. Bishop de la Hailandière discouraged her from completing these visits and later outright forbid her to do so. He wanted all missions in his diocese to be under his jurisdiction and control. He did not want her to influence the sisters in any way.

If the bishops did not approve the Rule for the Sisters of Providence, Mother Theodore knew that the sisters would be forced to move to an area where another bishop worked with them. This possibility made Bishop de la Hailandière increasingly more agitated and unpredictable with time.

The conflict between him and Mother Theodore came to a climax on May 20, 1847. When Mother Theodore went to visit the bishop, he immediately jumped into a tirade, accusing her of a list of irrational offenses. He threatened Mother Theodore's expulsion from the order if she did not comply with his unreasonable demands. He even threatened her with excommunication from the Catholic Church. Mother Theodore replied that the matter of her removal from the office of superior general needed to be presented to the sisters for a vote. The bishop walked out of the reception room and locked Mother Theodore inside. He refused to allow her to notify the sisters of her whereabouts.

The following day some of the sisters went to the rectory to check on her. The bishop proceeded to his reception room and unlocked the door. Mother Theodore fell to her knees and asked the bishop for his blessing. He complied with her request and motioned her out.

That evening he went to the convent in Vincennes where Mother Theodore stayed. The bishop said she no longer held the position of superior and was no longer a member of the Sisters of Providence. He demanded that she leave the diocese in disgrace.

He didn't even allow her to write to her sisters at Saint Mary-of-the-Woods.

The devoted chaplain at Saint Mary-of-the-Woods, Father John B. Corbe, wrote to Mother Theodore, begging her to come home regardless of the bishop's decision. He said that the situation deeply troubled the sisters. He argued that if the bishop released her from her vows, she could come to the community as a layperson, free to do as she wished.

All of the stress resulting from the years of the bishop's difficult disposition finally took its toll on Mother Theodore, and she became seriously ill with pleurisy. She remained bedridden at the convent in Vincennes. In addition, the clergy bore their own struggles with this bishop. Two years prior, as a result of his disagreements with so many people, Bishop de la Hailandière submitted his resignation, but Pope Gregory XVI did not accept it. As tensions increased within the diocese, however, word came on May 30 that Rome finally accepted the bishop's resignation.

In the interim between the bishop's resignation and the consecration of a new bishop, Father Corbe acted as temporary authority over the Sisters of Providence of Indiana. Father Corbe asked Mother Theodore to return home. This greatly relieved Mother Theodore and the sisters, as well as the clergy in the diocese. Months later the loving presence of Bishop John Stephan Bazin replaced Bishop de la Hailandière.

Still, after everything Bishop de la Hailandière put Mother Theodore through, she made no negative remarks about him. She modeled for the sisters that his position of authority entitled respect. She said that the bishop meant well. He was to be remembered in their prayers.

Mother Theodore wrote to Bishop Bouvier in France, "It appears that Bishop de la Hailandière has gone. His sacrifice has cost him much. He is very unhappy. I entreat you to pray for him."

The Forgiveness You Give and Receive

No matter how deeply wounded, Mother Theodore forgave completely and from the bottom of her heart. Her limitless level of forgiveness followed the teachings of Jesus found in Scripture. She readily granted forgiveness and understanding to those who harmed her. She quickly took responsibility for her actions, apologized, and asked for forgiveness.

We are saved by the forgiveness of our sins. We want and need this total absolution, but giving it to others isn't so easy. Typically we say we forgive, and then we recall the hurt caused us. We concentrate on our own feelings rather than seek forgiveness for the part we played in any given situation.

Holiness begins with forgiveness. If we want to be a saint we must ask forgiveness from people we have hurt and extend the gift we received from Jesus to those who offend us.

THREE WAYS TO FOLLOW
SAINT MOTHER THEODORE AND

FORGIVE LIKE JESUS

1. Think of the times you said or did something hurtful to someone. Ask for forgiveness in person or by writing a letter or email to them.

2. Talk to or write someone who hurt you, and let them know that you forgive them. Try your best to put the incident behind you, truly forgiving and forgetting.

3. Reflect on the Ten Commandments and think of how you broke one or more of them. Participate in the next opportunity to receive the Sacrament of Reconciliation, or if it is not available for some time, ask a priest if he will hear your confession.

Do nothing from selfish ambition or conceit, but in humility regard others as better than yourselves. Let each of you look not to your own interests, but to the interests of others. Let the same mind be in you that was in Christ Jesus.

—Philippians 2:3-5

Principle #7
Strive for Humility

Jesus entered this world in a most unassuming way. The greatest person to ever walk this earth was born into a modest family, laid in a straw bed, and surrounded by field animals in a strange town. He continued to live his life in such a manner, void of any form of luxury.

Jesus showed us by his example how to live humbly. He did not take on an authoritative position. He extended kindness to everyone including those considered untouchable. He ate with lepers and tax collectors. He spoke with women and children. He treated all of them with humility and as brothers and sisters.

Humility sets aside our pride and allows us to serve God and others. When we are humble, the focus of our efforts isn't on ourselves and our personal wants or likes: The first concern is to serve God and the people around us.

Sister Basilide tried Mother Theodore's patience on many occasions. She caused a little-known incident that resulted in Mother Theodore's name being written in all the local newspapers in connection with a troubling report. Mother Theodore responded to Sister Basilide that she didn't feel angry but rather humiliated. She quickly added that her reaction to public humiliation proved her own lack of humility. She used the situation as an opportunity to recognize her shortcomings and apologize to her subordinate.

Mother Theodore strove to live a life of humility. She made a conscious effort to control her ego. She admitted her faults and asked for forgiveness. She acknowledged her weaknesses in comparison to people she perceived as more perfect rather than proudly announce how she exceeded the state of her peers.

In this way Mother Theodore sought to learn how she could improve. Her perspective on the piety of Sister Francis offers an example. In regard to her friend she said, "Really, I am humiliated in seeing her run in the way of perfection while I just drag along." As holy and good as Mother Theodore was, this saint realized she could do better.

A Humble and Obedient Servant

Mother Theodore found the concept of obedience to be counter to the American way of life and challenging for the incoming sisters. She asked a priest in Madison, Wisconsin, to pray for the formation of the postulant he sent to Saint Mary-of-the-Woods. "It is difficult for many to understand the necessity of religious obedience," she said. "Especially does this seem to be the case in this country where the spirit of independence is carried into everything."

Today's society attaches a negative connotation to words such as obedience and submission. The words seem to encourage the mindless following of authority. But without obedience, there is chaos. The world needs laws in order to maintain peace. Wisdom is found in whom we obey—and why.

The word "obedience" comes from the Latin *obaudir*, which means "to listen" or "to hear with careful attention." When we obey God's commandments we submit and respond from a point of faith. We answer God's call by contemplating the direction we are being encouraged to take and then proceed out of our trust in God.

Scripture tells us that when we listen to God we will be rewarded. God told Abraham that he extended blessings to all of Abraham's descendants because Abraham obeyed God's voice (Genesis 22:15-19). The grace bestowed upon Abraham carried on for generations.

God in the person of Jesus repeated this message but with more urgency. Jesus said that our salvation depends upon obedience. "Not everyone who says to me, 'Lord, Lord,' will enter the kingdom of heaven, but only one who does the will of my Father in heaven" (Matthew 7:21).

Mother Theodore didn't find obedience to be difficult. She chose to submit to God and her mother superiors, bishops, pastors and chaplain. She affirmed her decision by her actions from the simple act of signing her letters to the clergy with "your very humble and devoted servant" and "your very humble and obedient servant." She placed herself at their feet.

When the mother superior sent Mother Theodore to Soulaines, the transfer clearly indicated a demotion, yet she reacted humbly. She said, "It is well for me, O Lord, that Thou hast humbled me." She responded to her new assignment with silent obedience.

Mother Theodore complied freely. It was not a thoughtless reaction to a command. Nor did her obedience or submission disregard her own gifts from God or her obligation to care for the God-given gifts of her body, mind and spirit.

Humility, the Foundation of the Virtues

We know that to be canonized a saint a candidate is required to practice the Virtues in their daily thoughts and actions. You may remember that the Church notes three theological virtues (faith, hope and charity) and four cardinal virtues (prudence, justice, fortitude and temperance). These virtues are based on humility, the desire to serve God and others before ourselves.

We can identify each one of these virtues in Mother Theodore, because they are tied into the principles by which she lived:

❖ **Faith.** Faith is the belief and trust in God and God's mercy. Mother Theodore's powerful faith in God is evident. Her faith kept her sailing through both physical and emotional storms. She did her best to spread that faith through the teachings of the scriptures.

❖ **Hope.** Hope is the result of faith. It is an assurance in our salvation. We are encouraged through hope to carry the cross of Christ and trust in our eternal life with God. Mother Theodore never lost hope because of her tremendous faith in God's providential love and the assurance that saints and angels surrounded her. She trusted the outcome of every situation to God's will and joyfully submitted to it.

❖ **Charity.** Mother Theodore showed evidence of charity in her generosity with her possessions, talents and time in the pursuit of the fair and just treatment of all people. She sought forgiveness for the pain she caused and generously extended that gift of forgiveness to the people in her life. She took Saint Paul's advice to heart: "As God's chosen ones, holy and beloved, clothe yourselves with compassion, kindness, humility, meekness and patience" (Colossians 3:12).

✤ **Prudence.** Mother Theodore fully understood the consequences of her actions and controlled her conduct accordingly. She spoke carefully when frustrated or upset. She advised, "Never speak when you are excited. Keep back the words that would wound your loving Jesus." She did not want to return a hurt with a hurtful remark. Mother Theodore wisely counseled, "It would be better to be guarded in your words than always asking pardon." She preferred to avoid infractions that required an apology. However, in the event she failed to do so, she quickly apologized.

✤ **Justice.** Love, mercy and justice were Mother Theodore's mantras. She sought the fair and equal treatment of the children and the sisters in her care on both sides of the Atlantic Ocean. She also sought the equality of all people regardless of gender or ethnicity.

✤ **Fortitude.** Mother Theodore's unstoppable approach helped her to overcome tremendous obstacles in order to accomplish the work God set before her. She dedicated her life to serving God and spreading the teachings of Jesus. She persevered through devastating fires, financial instability, and crippling ill health.

❖ **Temperance.** Mother Theodore lived a life of moderation and humility in the way of all good religious. As a religious woman she wore the modest habit covering all but her face and hands. She ate a bland diet due to her poor digestive condition and lived in the most basic housing.

Modest Spending Habits

Mother Theodore was frugal in her spending habits. Situations sometimes forced her to use credit, but she preferred to wait until she obtained the sufficient funds to make purchases. This caused one of the many points of contention between her and Bishop de la Hailandière. The bishop wanted to aggressively build on the property, resulting in significant debt. Even when she did comply with the bishop's instructions, Mother Theodore kept expenses to a minimum.

Before her death, Mother Theodore built a new convent to accommodate the growing community. She questioned her judgment in the building's design because she said it seemed like a castle to her, despite the assurances of the bishop that it certainly did not. She preferred not to promote anything that interfered with the community's vow of poverty.

In fact, the house was quite plain. No electricity, steam heat, or water ran through the building. The sisters used coal oil lamps and candles for light, and fireplaces and stoves for heat. They brought water in from outside wells. The sisters moved into the house before completion; Mother Theodore wrote to Father Martin on January of 1854 that she needed to stop writing to him because the ink and her fingers were frozen. At that time no windows or doors shielded the house from the outside elements.

Mother Theodore required few comforts. She contented herself with her mission rather than personal wants. She told the sisters not to dwell on their own happiness. They entered the religious life to accomplish God's will; they should occupy their thoughts with only the desire to please God.

When a sister told Mother Theodore that she felt more at home in her new location, Mother Theodore acknowledged the sister's satisfaction. However, she said, "a good religious never asks herself whether she is pleased or not. She is always satisfied where God wishes her to be."

Mother Theodore counseled the sisters to concentrate on their mission. "Never stop to ask yourself whether this or that pleases you, whether it is agreeable or not. Oh, no! But say to yourself; My God, you wish me to apply myself to this, or to that. I will do it for love of You with all the perfection of which I am capable. Then put yourself at the work whether you like it or not."

Humbled Herself for the Community

Mother Theodore was unpretentious. She did not lord her position of authority over her subordinates. She treated every individual regardless of age or class as a person of dignity and value. She believed God positioned her as an instrument in God's plan, and therefore did not seek personal recognition for her accomplishments. She didn't strive to excel for her own esteem but to complete her divine assignment. "What would it avail you to do better than someone else if it is from the motive of being admired? God would say to you at the last day, 'You have already received your reward, you have not worked for Me, I owe you nothing.'"

When Mother Mary sent Mother Theodore into the American wilderness, Mother Theodore invested her energies into the mission rather than focus on her frustration. She didn't completely agree with the vision of her superiors to establish a community in the middle of a forest, but she complied without argument or dissatisfaction.

She originally understood the Indiana mission to be a thriving city in the Diocese of Vincennes, with a surplus of students awaiting the opening of a school, and an existing building for use as a convent. She also expected the motherhouse in Ruillé to send postulants and funding until the new mission stood on its own.

The reality of it all was quite the contrary. She found her companions and herself abandoned in the dense, untamed woods of the Midwestern prairie. Her existence, and that of everyone else she took under her wings, depended on their own survival skills. If she didn't possess such tremendous humility to submit completely to God's Providence, she never could have succeeded.

The new community struggled the first few years, to say the least. When their financial progress suddenly went up in smoke with the fire of 1842, Bishop de la Hailandière urged Mother Theodore to return to France and request financial assistance from her motherhouse in Ruillé, the bishop of Le Mans, as well as friends, family, and anyone else who might help. He told her to explain about the fire, the loss of supplies and equipment, the heavy debts incurred, and the number of children who came to the school unable to pay tuition.

The series of difficulties left Saint Mary-of-the-Woods in a critical financial situation. Sister Olympiade wrote that while Mother Theodore solicited funds in France, the sisters ate a frugal breakfast and nothing else the rest of the day. The religious community asked the neighbors for eggs, cornmeal or potatoes. Few were in a position to help. The generosity of the widow, Priscilla Thralls, literally saved them from starvation. Mrs. Thralls kindly gave the community four of the six hills of potatoes from her winter supply.

Mother Theodore did not feel that begging for support from her French friends was beneath her. She begged on other occasions for previous parishes in which she served. She did not feel ashamed to admit the community's need for assistance. Unfortunately, when she returned to France, she found her native country in the middle of its own difficulties. There was little extra money to share.

Ruillé did not send postulants either. Mother Mary said the short supply there didn't meet the demands in her own country. Only three postulants came from France. Sister Francis Xavier originally volunteered to go with the first group but became too ill to travel until the following year. The other two were Mother Theodore's nieces, Sister Mary Theodore, and her sister Sister Frances Le Touzé, who joined the community in Indiana in 1854.

Practical Devotion

Mother Theodore exuded great devotion but with a sense of practicality. She didn't worry whether she accomplished enough on any given day. She just kept working the best way that she knew. She said she couldn't give God what God didn't give her. If a task needed to be done, she knew with confidence that God provides the ability and time to complete it.

More significantly, she did not take her devotional life to the extreme. She clearly understood the meaning of humility. She maintained a balance between the highest regard for the needs of others without compromising her own mental and physical health. She didn't see any holiness in neglecting oneself in the pursuit of caring for others.

When Mother Theodore learned of the illness of Sister Vincent, she wrote to the chaplain, Father Kundek, asking why Sister Vincent went out in frigid weather. "I do not approve of that kind of fervor," Mother Theodore wrote. "It is not fervor at all, but real imprudence. Scold her, I beg of you."

Mother Theodore also expressed her disappointment with the behavior of young Sister Josephine. She loved Sister Josephine since the first day she came to the Academy. Sister Josephine neglected her health and died suddenly. Mother Theodore reacted with sadness and frustration. She told the other sisters that their health belonged to God. She said, "You ought to take reasonable care of yourselves, so as to preserve a life which is entirely devoted to God and to the souls He loves so much." She continued saying that Sister Josephine concealed her sufferings, and not complaining when one is sick did not result in any real merit or humility. Mother Theodore insisted that the sisters stop to care for themselves so they might recover quickly and get back to work.

She also believed that acts of piety must be done within reason. On one occasion, Sister Mary James informed Mother Theodore that she went to confession twice a week. Mother Theodore questioned the purpose of such an excessive practice. If Sister Mary James repeatedly did something for which she needed to confess, the solution was to break the bad habit—not confess the same sin over and over!

Mother Theodore also advised against fasting when the sisters barely got enough food on a regular basis and needed the energy to do the required physical labor. "If you think in conscience that you can fast without becoming exhausted, I permit you to do so: but if you perceive that you suffer too much from it, that you are weak and sick, you must not continue."

Joy and Humor

Mother Theodore enjoyed the simple pleasures in life. She happily cherished all of God's creations, from the sunrise sparkling on the ocean to the most intolerant individual with whom she worked. She valued every person and every thing. She felt rich in the blessings of the Lord.

The sisters also recognized her wonderful sense of humor. Mother Theodore laughed quickly at herself and at situations others might find troubling. She once joked that Sister Francis and she were so feeble that together they didn't amount to two cents.

Her sense of fun showed evidence in her diaries as well. In one entry she wrote of the storms on her first ocean voyage to America. With wind howling, the clanging of pots, pans and dishes in the lower deck, and fierce turbulence hurling the sisters about their cabin, she described how they struggled to keep a candle lit. Mother Theodore also wrote how Sister Liguori nearly killed her when the turbulence flung the sister against her with all her weight. "Never did we laugh so heartily as that evening," she said.

She showed her playfulness in her guidance also. When Sister Maria feared losing her mind, Mother Theodore told her not to trouble herself over thinking that way. After all, she responded, "We can't lose what we never had."

She also used images that surprised and amused. She said it was best to put troubling situations behind us. Complaining about, discussing, or repeatedly worrying over the same things is not healthy. "The more we stir up a dung-hill the more it exhales bad odors."

She even joked about the best attributes of her dear friend. Sister Francis devoted her life to teaching catechism to young people. She worked tirelessly in spite of suffering from chronic ill health. Mother Theodore teased that her friend would spend her last breath promoting the faith. The only way to know if Sister Francis truly died would be to bring a young boy to her room to ask for preparation of Baptism or First Communion and see if she responded. "If she opens neither her eyes nor her mouth, we may have the funeral in all safety," she laughed.

Your Efforts to be Humble

Mother Theodore definitely put the respect and dignity of other people before herself. Her thoughts centered on the happiness of others, and she advised her sisters to do the same. She honored Scripture by doing nothing from selfish ambition.

We find the twofold theme with humility, just as seen with several of the other principles. In securing our just and fair treatment we are to see that the same treatment is awarded to all people; we are forgiven to the extent that we forgive; we lead by serving. In this same manner, we are exalted when we are humble.

Humility is one of the most challenging of all Mother Theodore's principles to attain. It requires our constant and honest self-assessment in controlling the impulse to satisfy our own desires before anyone else's. This is contrary to our culture, which often focuses on the quickest ways to achieve self-gratification.

We can move toward a more humble life by taking small steps, whether we're striving to be more understanding, apologetic, or less concerned about getting credit for our efforts. Such sacrifice does not go unnoticed. Jesus said, "For all who exalt themselves will be humbled, and those who humble themselves will be exalted" (Luke 14:11).

THREE WAYS TO FOLLOW
SAINT MOTHER THEODORE AND

STRIVE FOR HUMILITY

1. Think back on situations where you feel someone hurt
   you, and now make an effort to understand it from the
   other person's point of view. How did they perceive
   what happened? How did you offend them? Apologize
   to them for the pain you caused.

2. Avoid all gossip via telephone, email, the Internet, or in
   person. If you are sent a message, or told something that
   demeans or damages someone else's reputation, tell the
   person who sent the message that you are uncomfortable
   receiving that type of information and will not accept it
   in the future. Also, be certain not to send any offensive
   information or spread gossip.

3. Eagerly acknowledge the achievements of others. When
   a family member, neighbor or coworker performs an act
   of kindness or accomplishes even a small achievement,
   be sure to take the time to recognize a job well done.

And if I have prophetic powers, and understand all mysteries and have all knowledge, and if I have faith, so as to remove mountains, but do not have love, I am nothing. If I give away all my possessions, and if I hand over my body so that I may boast, but do not have love, I gain nothing.

—1 Corinthians 13:2-3

Conclusion
Following Saint Mother Theodore

Mother Theodore offers a timeless example of holiness because she set a standard for herself based on the basic principles of Christianity. She lived her life by the teachings of Jesus and turned herself over entirely to God.

In the 1904 publication, *Life and Life—Work of Mother Theodore Guérin*, Sister Mary Theodosia Mug wrote this observation of Mother Theodore: "Providence ordained her to be a light set upon the mountain, whose brilliancy would be a guide to future generations." We are approaching two centuries since her death, and Mother Theodore continues to inspire us and light a path for us to follow.

So much may be gained through our efforts to live like Mother Theodore. If we seek justice for the people we encounter, extend the gift of forgiveness, and spread the Word to them, we move toward the advancement of peace and love in the world. Should we need help along the way, we have the saints and angels on which to call.

More so, we have a loving God who hears our pleas. Perhaps most admirable about Mother Theodore was her incredible faith and trust in divine Providence. No matter how grave her circumstances may have been, God was first and foremost in her life, as God should be in ours.

Mother Theodore's love for God extended to all of God's creations. Her life was rich with people to love and who loved her. Her many friends extended across both sides of the Atlantic Ocean, from one continent to another. She dearly cared for the sisters and all those connected to Saint Mary-of-the-Woods. She especially loved the children. Repeatedly she counseled the sisters to love the children first, and then teach. This great love of hers is a key to her sanctity, for we can have faith powerful enough to move mountains, but it is nothing without love (1 Corinthians 13:2).

You can live and love as Mother Theodore did. You too can be a saint, or at the very least, strive to be holy. If you ask, God will give you the strength to do so. And you can ask Saint Mother Theodore for help along the way. If you haven't already noticed, she was an incredible woman and a fine example for you to follow on your own road to heaven.

To learn more about Saint Mother Theodore Guérin, read her biography, *The Eighth American Saint*, by Katherine Burton, or her own writings found in *Journals and Letters of Mother Theodore Guérin*.

Timeline of the Life and Canonization of Saint Mother Theodore Guérin

1797	Birth of Mother Theodore's brother, Jean-Laurent.
1798	October 2: Birth of Mother Theodore Guérin. Born in the village of Etables-sur-Mer in Brittany, France, to Laurent and Isabelle Guérin. She was baptized Anne-Thérèse.
1800	Death of Mother Theodore's three-year-old brother, Jean-Laurent.
1803	Birth of Mother Theodore's sister, Marie-Jeanne.
1806	Father Dujarie began recruiting young women to teach and care for the children of France.
	Birth of John Corbe, future chaplain of Saint Mary-of-the-Woods, in the diocese of Rennes, Brittany, France.
1808	Mother Theodore received her First Communion.
1809	Birth of Mother Theodore's brother, Laurent-Marie.
1813	Death of Mother Theodore's brother, Laurent-Marie.

1813 or 1814	Death of Mother Theodore's father, Laurent Guérin.
1820	Father Dujarie's group of women received recognition as the religious congregation, the Sisters of Providence. Mother Marie Madeleine du Roscoät elected superior general.
1822	Mother Mary Lecor elected superior general after the death of Mother Marie Madeleine.
1823	August 18: Mother Theodore entered the congregation of the Sisters of Providence at Ruillé-sur-Loir, France. Her superior gave her the name of Sister Saint Theodore.
1825	September 8: Mother Theodore, then known as Sister Saint Theodore, professed her first vows and received the religious habit. She was assigned to the parish in Preuilly-sur-Claise, France.
1826	Mother Theodore transferred to the Saint Aubin parish in Rennes and appointed superior.

November 19: Royal decree approved the congregation of the Sisters of Providence, granting it legal existence as a corporation. |
| 1831 | September 5: Mother Theodore professed her perpetual vows.

Mother Saint Charles Jolle elected superior general. |
| 1834 | Mother Theodore transferred from Rennes and appointed superior of the parish school at Soulaines, France. |

1835	Mother Mary Lecor elected superior general again. She served until her retirement in 1871.
1836	Reverend Stanislaus Buteux appointed chaplain of Saint Mary-of-the-Woods, Indiana, serving until 1839.
1839	May 12: Death of Mother Theodore's mother, Isabelle.
	Vicar general Reverend Célestine de la Hailandière went to France in search of women religious to establish schools in America in the Vincennes, Indiana, diocese.
	August 18: Reverend de la Hailandière was consecrated the bishop of Vincennes after the death of Bishop Simon Bruté.
1840	July 27: Mother Theodore and her companions departed France for the ocean voyage to New York.
	September 4: Mother Theodore and her companions arrived in the United States of America at the harbor in New York, New York.
	October 22: Mother Theodore and her companions arrived at Saint Mary-of-the-Woods, Indiana.
1841	July 4: The Academy at Saint Mary-of-the-Woods, also referred to as Saint Mary's Academy for Young Ladies, opened its doors.
1842	Devastating fire at Saint Mary-of-the-Woods consumed the barn with approximately 150 bushels of oats, hay, corn and farm implements.

1843	The bank in Illinois with all the Sisters of Providence's money failed, losing everything they had.
	Mother Theodore went to France to seek funding.
1844	Mother Theodore returned from France.
1845	Bishop de la Hailandière submitted his resignation. The resignation was not accepted by Pope Gregory XVI.
1846	The Sisters of Providence of Saint Mary-of-the-Woods incorporated its institution with the State of Indiana. The sisters were already naturalized citizens of the United States.
1847	January 29: Death of Sister Mary Liguori (Louise) Tiercin.
	Resignation of Bishop de la Hailandière accepted in Rome.
	October 24: Consecration of The Reverend John Stephen Bazin as the new bishop of the Vincennes, Indiana, Diocese.
1848	April 23: Death of Bishop John Stephen Bazin.
	Consecration of the Right Reverend Maurice de Saint Palais as bishop of the Vincennes, Indiana, Diocese.
1849	The Sisters of Providence opened two orphanages in Vincennes to care for the orphans of the cholera outbreak.

1854	Mother Theodore's nieces arrived in the United States to enter the community of the Sisters of Providence of Saint Mary-of-the-Woods, Indiana.
1855	Death of Mother Theodore's friend and mentor, Bishop Bouvier of Le Mans, France.
1856	Death of Sister Saint Francis Xavier.
	May 14: Death of Mother Theodore Guérin.
1877	Sister Mary Theodosia Mug graduated from the Academy at Saint Mary-of-the-Woods.
	Death of Marie-Jeanne, Mother Theodore's sister.
1888	Sister Mary Theodosia Mug entered the Sisters of Providence.
1906	Sister Mary Theodosia Mug had a mastectomy after a diagnosis of breast cancer.
1907	December 3: The remains of Mother Theodore were transferred from the Sisters of Providence Cemetery to the crypt in the Church of the Immaculate Conception, Saint Mary-of-the-Woods, Indiana.
1908	October 30: Miraculous healing of Sister Mary Theodosia Mug with the intercession of Mother Theodore.
1909	September 8: The Cause for the Beatification and Canonization of Mother Theodore was opened by Bishop Francis Silas Chatard of the Diocese of Indianapolis.

1913	June 30: The Informative Process concluded.
1927	July 25: The Congregation for the Causes of Saints approved the writings of Mother Theodore.
1937	Interviews and study for the process continued in the Diocese of Saint Brieuc and Le Mans, France.
1955	December 6: Cardinals at the Vatican voted to continue the Cause.
1956	February 19: Pope Pius XII approved and signed the *Placet Eugenio* to continue the Cause. The Apostolic Process of the Cause was formally introduced.
1956 -1958	Archbishop Paul C. Schulte of the Archdiocese of Indianapolis presided over the Apostolic Process and conducted meetings at Saint Mary-of-the-Woods and Indianapolis, Indiana.
1988	May 12: Vatican historical consultants voted unanimously to approve the Positio, the study of Mother Theodore's life and virtues. The approval affirmed that the information was sufficient to judge the sanctity of Mother Theodore.
1992	February 15: Vatican theologians approved the *Positio*.
	July 22: Pope John Paul II granted Mother Theodore the title "Venerable" indicating that she lived a virtuous life to a heroic degree.

1996	November 20: Vatican medical consultants unanimously approved the healing of Sister Mary Theodosia Mug through the intercession of Mother Theodore as a miracle.
1997	March 25: Vatican theologians unanimously approved the cure of Sister Mary Theodosia Mug through the intercession of Mother Theodore as a miracle.
	June 3: Cardinals unanimously approved the cure of Sister Mary Theodosia Mug through the intercession of Mother Theodore as a miracle.
	July 7: Pope John Paul II accepted the healing of Sister Mary Theodosia Mug through the intercession of Mother Theodore as a miracle.
1998	October 25: During a beatification ceremony in Saint Peter's Square at the Vatican, Pope John Paul II granted the title "Blessed" to Mother Theodore indicating that she was a holy woman worthy of honor and veneration.
2003	A formal trial was held in the Archdiocese of Indianapolis to determine the validity of the claims of the healing of Philip McCord through the intercession of Mother Theodore to be a miracle.
2005	June 9: Evidence of a miracle granted to Philip McCord through Mother Theodore's intercession was approved by a commission of medical examiners appointed by the Congregation for the Causes of Saints in Rome.

November 20: Evidence of the miracle granted to Philip McCord through Mother Theodore's intercession was approved by a commission of theologians appointed by the Congregation for the Causes of Saints in Rome.

2006

February 21: The Holy See's Congregation for the Causes of Saints affirmed the curing of Philip McCord's eye ailment to be a miracle that occurred through the intercession of Mother Theodore.

April: Pope Benedict signed a decree affirming the findings of the congregation for the Causes of Saints regarding the miraculous healing of Philip McCord.

October 15: Canonization of Mother Theodore Guérin in Saint Peter's Square, Vatican City, Italy.

October 21, 22: Weekend celebration for the canonization of Mother Theodore and Foundation Day held at Saint Mary-of-the-Woods, Indiana.

October 3   **Feast Day of Saint Mother Theodore Guérin**

Mother Theodore's Favorite Prayers

Memorare

Remember, O most gracious Virgin Mary, that never was it known that anyone who fled to your protection, implored your help or sought your intercession was left unaided. Inspired by this confidence, I fly to you, O virgin of virgins, my mother. To you I come. Before you I stand, sinful and sorrowful. O mother of the Word incarnate, despise not my petitions but in your mercy, hear and answer me. Amen.

Pater Noster/Our Father

Our Father, who art in heaven, hallowed be thy name. Thy kingdom come. Thy will be done on earth as it is in heaven. Give us this day our daily bread, and forgive us our trespasses, as we forgive those who trespass against us, and lead us not into temptation, but deliver us from evil. Amen.

Te Deum

O God, we praise you. We acknowledge you to be the Lord. Everlasting Father, all the earth worships you. To you all the angels, the heavens and all the powers, all the cherubim and seraphim, unceasingly proclaim, holy, holy, holy Lord God of hosts! Heaven and earth are full of the majesty of your glory. The glorious choir of the apostles, the wonderful company of prophets, the white-robed army of martyrs, praise you. Holy church throughout the world acknowledges you, the Father of infinite majesty, your adorable, true and only son, and the Holy Spirit, the comforter. O Christ, you are the king of glory! You are the everlasting Son of the Father. You, having taken it upon yourself to deliver man, did not disdain the virgin's womb. You overcame the sting of death and have opened to believers the kingdom of heaven. You sit at the right hand of God, in the glory of the Father. We believe that you will come to be our judge. We beseech you, therefore, to help your servants whom you have redeemed with your precious blood. Make them to be numbered with your saints in everlasting glory.

V. Save your people, O Lord, and bless their inheritance!

R. Govern them, and raise them up forever.

V. Every day we thank you.

R. And we praise your name forever, yes, forever and ever.

V. O Lord, deign to keep us from sin this day.

R. Have mercy on us, O Lord, have mercy on us.

V. Let your mercy, O Lord, be upon us, for we have hoped in you.

R. O Lord, in you I have hoped. Let me never be put to shame.

Stabat Mater

At the cross her station keeping,
Stood the mournful mother weeping,
Close to Jesus to the last

Through her heart, his sorrow sharing,
All his bitter anguish bearing,
Now at length the sword had passed.

Oh how sad and sore distressed
Was that mother highly blessed
Of the sole-begotten one!

Christ above in torment hangs,
She beneath beholds the pangs
Of her dying, glorious son.

Is there one who would not weep
Whelmed in miseries so deep
Christ's dear mother to behold?

Can the human heart refrain
From partaking in her pain,
In that mother's pain untold?

Bruised, derided, cursed, defiled,
She beheld her tender child,
All with bloody scourges rent,

For the sins of his own nation
Saw him hang in desolation
Till his spirit forth he sent.

O thou mother, fount of love,
Touch my spirit from above.
Make my heart with thine accord:

Make me feel as thou hast felt:
Make my soul to glow and melt
With the love of Christ, my Lord.

Holy mother pierce me through.
In my heart each wound renew
Of my savior crucified.

Let me share with thee his pain,
Who for all our sins was slain,
Who for me in torments died.

Let me mingle tears with thee.
Mourning him who mourned for me,
All the days that I may live.

By the cross with thee to stay,
There with thee to weep and pray,
Is all I ask of thee to give.

Virgin of all virgins best
Listen to my fond request:
Let me share thy grief divine:

Let me, to my latest breath,
In my body hear the death
Of that dying son of thine.

Wounded with his every wound,
Steep my soul till it hath swooned
In his very blood away;

Be to me, O virgin, nigh,
Lest in flames I burn and die,
In his awful judgment day.

Christ, when thou shalt call me hence,
Be thy mother my defense,
Be thy cross my victory;

While my body here decays
May my soul thy goodness praise,
Safe in paradise with thee.

Amen.

V. Pray for us, virgin most sorrowful.
R. That we may be made worthy of the promises of Christ

Let us pray
Grant, we beseech thee, O Lord Jesus Christ, that the most
Blessed Virgin Mary, thy mother, through whose most holy soul,
in the hour of thine own passion, the sword of sorrow passed,
may intercede for us before, the throne of thy mercy, now and
at the hour of our death, through thee, Jesus Christ, savior of
the world, who livest and reignest, with the Father and the Holy
Ghost, now and forever. Amen.

The Rosary

Mother Theodore had a great devotion to Mary—the Blessed Mother—and praying the rosary. The rosary is a form of meditation based on repetitive prayer and a focus on mysteries, which are some of the basic truths of our Christian faith.

An explanation on how it is prayed with all the prayers is too lengthy to print here. For a complete and easy way to pray the rosary, see the book, *The Rosary Prayer by Prayer* available from ACTA Publications. With this book you can pray the rosary by following along page-by-page.

Glossary

Academy: Also called Saint Mary's Academy for Young Ladies and Saint Mary's Female Institute. Founded on July 4, 1841, by Mother Theodore and the Sisters of Providence. Now known as Saint Mary-of-the-Woods College, the oldest liberal arts college for women in the United States.

Adoration: Perpetual adoration is the continuous exposition of the Blessed Sacrament which offers an opportunity to focus prayer on the glory and goodness of God.

Anne-Thérèse: Mother Theodore's baptismal name.

Apostolic Process of the Cause: The steps to be taken before formally declaring someone a saint.

Bailly, SP, Mary Cecilia (Eleanor): Sister of Providence who arrived at Saint Mary-of-the-Woods in November of 1841. Elected to the position of mother superior following the death of Mother Theodore.

Bazin, The Right Reverend John Stephen: Bishop of the Vincennes, Indiana Diocese from October 1847 until his death in April 1848.

Beatification: A process, guided by the Vatican's Congregation for the Causes of Saints that begins with an intense investigation of a deceased person's life, writings and virtues. Proof of one miracle through the intercession of the candidate is required except in the case of martyrs. If the person meets all the requirements, the pope gives the person the title "Blessed" and decrees that he or she may be honored.

Blessed: The title given to a person who has been beatified.

Blessed Sacrament: The consecrated host. The body of Christ.

Blessed Virgin Mary: Mary, the Mother of Jesus, also known by the names of Blessed Mother, the Virgin Mary, and hundreds of other terms of affection and devotion.

Bonaparte, Napoleon: French general who named himself emperor of France at the end of the French Revolution.

Bourbon, Marie-Amélie de: Last Queen of France. Wife of King Louis Philippe. Italian Princess and niece of Marie Antoinette. Friend of Mother Theodore and benefactor to the community of the Sisters of Providence of Saint Mary-of-the-Woods, Indiana.

Bouvier, The Most Reverend Jeane-Baptiste: 1783-1854. Bishop of Le Mans, France 1834-1854. Mentor and friend to Mother Theodore.

Boyer, SP, Olympiade (Therese): 1806-1893. Sister of Providence who accompanied Mother Theodore to the United States in 1840.

Bruté, Bishop Simon William Gabriel: First Bishop of Vincennes, Indiana. Consecrated on October 28, 1834, and served as bishop until his death in 1839.

Buteux, Reverend Stanislaus: Missionary from France who arrived in the United States in 1836. Appointed as first chaplain of Saint Mary-of-the-Woods, Indiana, until his removal in 1841.

Byerley, Samuel: Friend of Mother Theodore since their first meeting in New York in 1840.

Canonization: Papal declaration that a person who died as a martyr and/or who practiced Christian virtues to a heroic degree is with God and is worthy of honor and imitation.

Cardinal Virtues: The virtues of prudence, justice, temperance and fortitude.

Cause: The name given to the process of investigating, studying and promoting a person for beatification and canonization.

Charity: One of the three theological virtues.

Chartier, Reverend William: French Canadian missionary who accompanied Mother Theodore and her companions from Philadelphia to Indiana in 1840.

Cincinnati: The name of the ship on which Mother Theodore sailed to America in 1840.

Congregation for the Causes of Saints: Vatican delegation that is responsible for the process required for beatification and canonization and for the preservation of relics of holy people.

Corbe, Reverend John: 1805-1872. Chaplain of Saint Mary-of-the-Woods from 1842 to 1872. Ecclesiastical Superior and devoted friend to Mother Theodore and the Sisters of Providence in Indiana.

Decree: An official order issued by a pope and/or by an ecumenical council for the Roman Catholic Church.

Diocese of Vincennes: Area of the Catholic Church during the years of Mother Theodore's ministry in the United States that included all of Indiana and the eastern third of Illinois including the city of Chicago.

Doane, Sidney A.: Physician who welcomed and showed great kindness to Mother Theodore and the sisters upon their arrival in New York.

Dujarié, Reverend Jacques Francois: Founder of the Sisters of Providence in France.

Establishments of the Sisters of Providence: Missions opened by Mother Theodore that included the Academy at Saint Mary-of-the-Woods and schools at Jasper, Vincennes, Montgomery, Madison, Terre Haute, Fort Wayne, Evansville, North Madison, Lanesville and Columbus, Indiana; Saint Francisville, Illinois; two orphanages; and pharmacies at Vincennes and Saint Mary-of-the-Woods.

Etables, Brittany, France: Birthplace of Mother Theodore.

Eucharist: The sacrament and true presence of the body, blood and divinity of Jesus Christ under the appearance of bread and wine.

Evangelist: From the Greek *euangelistos*. One who announces the good news of Jesus Christ.

Faith: One of the three theological virtues. The belief and trust in the goodness of the loving God.

Fillmore, Millard: President of the United States from 1850 until 1853.

Forgiveness: The waiving or forgetting of an offense.

Fortitude: One of the four cardinal virtues. The strength to attain good even in the midst of insurmountable obstacles and suffering.

French Revolution: Pivotal point in French history from 1789-1799 when the monarchy was overthrown.

Gage, SP, Saint Vincent Ferrer (Victoire): 1800-1874. Sister of Providence accompanied Mother Theodore to the United States in 1840.

Guérin, Laurent: Father of Mother Theodore.

Guérin, Jean-Laurant: 1798-1800. Brother of Mother Theodore.

Guérin, Laurant-Marie: 1809-1812. Brother of Mother Theodore.

Guérin, Marie-Jeanne: 1807-1877. Sister of Mother Theodore. Later known as Madame Louis Barthélemy Le Touzé. Marie-Jeanne had two daughters who became Sisters of Providence and joined Mother Theodore in America at Saint Mary-of-the-Woods.

Guérin, SP, Saint Mother Theodore: 1798-1856. Sister of Providence named Sister Saint Theodore, later known as Mother Theodore Guérin. Founder of the Sisters of Providence of Saint Mary-of-the-Woods, Indiana, and Saint Mary-of-the-Woods College.

Habit: Clothing worn by members of a religious congregation as a sign of dedication to God.

Hailandière, Bishop Célestine-René-Laurent Guynemer de la: 1798-1882. Bishop of the Vincennes, Indiana, Diocese 1839 to 1847.

Harrison, William H: United States President in 1841.

Heroic Virtues: Includes the three theological virtues of faith, hope, and charity and the four cardinal virtues of prudence, justice, fortitude, and temperance.

Hope: One of the three theological virtues. Encouragement to carry on in the assurance of our salvation.

Humility: The practice of serving God's will and the well-being of others before oneself based on the understanding that one is indebted to God's mercy.

Immaculate Conception Church: Church located on the Saint Mary-of-the-Woods, Indiana campus and home to the shrine to Mother Theodore.

Ineffabilis Deus: Dogma of the Immaculate Conception stating that Mary was conceived without sin signed by Pope Pius IX on December 8, 1854.

Intercede: To make a request on behalf of another person.

Intercessory prayer: To ask a holy person to take a request to God.

Justice: One of the four cardinal virtues. The giving of rights and provisions due to other people.

Kundek, Reverend Joseph: 1810-1857. Friend of Mother Theodore and the Sisters of Providence. Austrian nobleman who became a missionary priest and the first resident pastor of Jasper, Indiana in 1838.

Lecacheur, Dr: Physician and teacher of medicine and pharmacy to Mother Theodore in Soulaines, France.

Lecor, Mother Mary (Aimée): Superior General of the Sisters of Providence in France 1822-31, 1835-1871.

LeFer de la Motte, SP, Saint Francis Xavier (Irma): 1816-1856. Sister of Providence. Arrived at Saint Mary-of-the-Woods in November of 1841. Close friend to Mother Theodore.

Lefevre, Isabelle: Maiden name of the mother of Mother Theodore.

Le Touzé, Madame Louis Barthélemy (Marie-Jeanne Guérin): 1807-1877. Sister of Mother Theodore.

Lerée, SP, Mary Xavier (Francis Louise): 1813-1897. Sister of Providence who accompanied Mother Theodore to the United States in 1840.

Liturgy: Public worship of the Church including the rites and ceremonies of the Mass and the sacraments.

Love: One of the three theological virtues. Also referred to as the virtue of charity.

Marescot, Countess de: Benefactor of the Sisters of Providence in France and the United States and friend to Mother Theodore.

Martyr: Person who decides to suffer and die rather than give up their faith or principles.

McCord, Philip: Employee of the Sisters of Providence and the second recipient of a miraculous cure after the intercession of Mother Theodore Guérin.

Memorare: Latin for "remember." Prayer to the Virgin Mary beginning with the words, "Remember most gracious Virgin Mary."

Mentor: One who shares knowledge, guidance, wisdom and contacts with the intention of promoting growth in another individual.

Miracles: Observable events or effects that cannot be explained by the laws of nature and are attributed to the direct action of God.

Miraculous Medal: A particular medal believed to be designed by the Blessed Virgin Mary and revealed to Saint Catherine Labore in Paris, France, in 1830.

Monstrance: An ornate vessel used to hold a consecrated host.

Mug, SP, Mary Theodosia: 1860-1943. Sister of Providence and recipient of the first miraculous healing attributed to Mother Theodore Guérin.

Novice: Woman in her second and third year of discernment in a religious congregation.

Novitiate: Period of preparation and formation of religious instruction during which the novice—the woman entering the community—and her superiors determine whether or not she is suitable for religious life.

Parmentier, Silvia: Friend and benefactor to Mother Theodore who warmly welcomed her upon her arrival in the United States.

Petition: Request or plea for assistance.

Pierce, Franklin: President of the United States from 1853 until 1857.

Polk, James K: President of the United States from 1845 until 1849.

Pope Blessed Pius IX: Pope during Mother Theodore's lifetime serving from 1846-78.

Pope Gregory XVI: Pope during Mother Theodore's lifetime serving from 1831-1846. Signed the dogma, *Ineffabilis Deus*.

Pope Leo XII: Pope during Mother Theodore's lifetime serving from 1823-29.

Pope Pius VI: Pope during Mother Theodore's lifetime serving from 1775-99.

Pope Pius VII: Pope during Mother Theodore's lifetime serving from 1800-23.

Pope Pius VIII: Pope during Mother Theodore's lifetime serving from 1829-1830.

Positio: Documented account of the life, work and writings of a holy person and candidate for canonization.

Postulant: Title generally given to a woman when she first enters a religious congregation.

Pray: To talk to God directly or through the intercession of holy people.

Preuilly-sur-Claise: Town where Mother Theodore was sent on her first assignment as a Sister of Providence.

Protégé: Recipient of a mentor's guidance.

Providence: God and God's wisdom and plan for creation.

Prudence: One of the four cardinal virtues. The act of discerning the true good in every circumstance.

Reconciliation: Contemporary term for the Sacrament of Penance. Effect of Christ's saving passion, death and resurrection.

Relics: Physical remains and effects of saints and martyrs. Relics are respected as sacred memorials of saints.

(A) Religious: Woman dedicated to serving God and belonging to a religious order.

Rennes, France: City where Mother Theodore served for eight years.

Roscoät, Mother Marie Madeleine (Julie Josephine Zoë) du: First superior general of the Sisters of Providence at Ruillé, France.

Ruille-sur-Loir: Town where the French motherhouse of the Sisters of Providence was located.

Rule: Constitution or guidelines for a religious congregation which expresses its ideals and commitments.

Stabat Mater: Traditional hymn often used at the Stations of the Cross. One of Mother Theodore's favorite prayers.

Saint: Title of honor and recognition given by the Church to someone who lived a holy life and is believed to be in heaven and capable of interceding with God.

Saint Anne: Mother of the Virgin Mary.

Saint Aubin Parish: Parish in Rennes, France, where Mother Theodore was assigned for eight years.

Saint Mary-of-the-Woods, Indiana: Town where Mother Theodore founded the motherhouse of the American Sisters of Providence and the Academy which is now known as Saint Mary-of-the-Woods College.

Saint Mary-of-the-Woods College: The Academy, also called Saint Mary's Academy for Young Ladies, founded on July 4, 1841, by Mother Theodore and the Sisters of Providence. The oldest liberal arts college for women in the United States.

Saint-Palais, The Right Reverend James Marie Maurice Landes D'Aussac de: 1811-1877. Fourth bishop of the Vincennes Diocese 1849-1877.

Scripture: Sacred writing, the Bible.

Sénéschal, SP, Basilide (Josephine): 1812-1878. Sister of Providence who accompanied Mother Theodore from France to the United States in 1840.

Sisters of Providence: Women religious order founded in France by the Reverend Jacques Francois Dujarié and Mother Marie Madeleine du Roscoät and in the United States by Mother Theodore Guérin.

Soulaines, France: City where Mother Theodore was assigned from 1834 until her departure for the United States in 1840.

Tabernacle: Receptacle in which the Blessed Sacrament is reserved.

Taylor, Zachary: President of the United States from 1849 until 1850.

Temperance: One of the four cardinal virtues. The moderation of sensual pleasures.

Theological Virtues: Includes the virtues of faith, hope and charity.

Thralls, Joseph and Sarah: Also known as Uncle Joe and Aunt Sallie. Owners of the farmhouse where Mother Theodore and her companions lived upon their arrival at Saint Mary-of-the-Woods, Indiana, in 1840. Longtime friends of the community.

Tiercin, SP, Mary Liguori (Louise): 1818-1847. Sister of Providence who accompanied Mother Theodore from France to the United States in 1840.

Tyler, John: President of the United States from 1841 until 1845.

Van Buren, Martin: President of the United States from 1837 until 1841.

Venerable: Title given to a person who lived a life of heroic virtues.

Venerate, veneration: Feelings of deep respect and honor for people who are with God in heaven.

Vincennes, Indiana: Area located on the Wabash River in southwestern Indiana.

Virtues: Exemplary characteristics including the cardinal virtues of prudence, justice, fortitude and temperance and the theological virtues of faith, hope and charity.

Vows: Promises made by members of religious congregations most often including the observation of poverty, chastity and obedience. First vows are made for a set period of time. Perpetual vows are to be observed for the remainder of one's life.

Bibliography

Brown, PhD., Sister Mary Borromeo. *The History of the Sisters of Providence of Saint Mary-of-the-Woods.* New York: Benziger Brothers, Inc., 1949.

Burton, Katherine. *Faith is the Substance. The Life of Mother Theodore Guerin Foundress of the Sisters of Providence of Saint Mary-Of-The-Woods, Indiana.* Saint Louis: B. Herder Book Co., 1959.

Burton, Katherine. *The Eighth American Saint. The Life of Saint Mother Theodore Guerin, Foundress of the Sisters of Providence of Saint Mary-of-the-Woods, Indiana.* Skokie, IL: ACTA Publications, 2007.

Covey, Stephen R. *Principle-Centered Leadership.* New York: Fireside, 1992.

Doyle, Mary K. *Mentoring Heroes.* Batavia, IL: 3E Press, 2000.

Gruver, Rebecca Brooks. *An American History.* New York: Newbery Award Records, Inc., 1985.

Guérin, Mother Theodore. *Journals and Letters of Mother Theodore Guerin. Foundress of the Sisters of Providence of Saint Mary-of-the-Woods Indiana.* Indiana: Saint Mary-of-the-Woods, 2005.

Huels, J.C.D., John M. *The Pastoral Companion. A Canon Law Handbook for Catholic Ministry.* Quincy, IL: Franciscan Press, 1995.

Joseph Eleanor, SP, Sister. *Call to Courage. A Story of Mother Theodore Guerin.* Notre Dame: Dujarie Press, 1968.

Knight, Kevin. *The Catholic Encyclopedia, Volume XIV.* New York: New Advent, 2006.

Libreria Editrice Vaticana. *Catechism of the Catholic Church.* Dubuque, IA: Brown-Roa, 1994.

McCutcheon, Marc. *The Writer's Guide to Everyday Life in the 1800s.* Cincinnati: Writer's Digest Books, 1993.

Mitchell, Penny Blaker. *Mother Theodore Guerin. A Woman for Our Time.* Saint Mary-of-the-Woods: Office of Congregational Advancement Sisters of Providence, 1998.

Mug, SP, Sister Mary Theodosia. *Life and Life-Work of Mother Theodore Guerin. Foundress of the Sisters of Providence at Saint Mary-of-the-Woods, Vigo County, IN.* New York: Benziger Brothers, 1904.

Sisters of Providence Saint Mary-of-the-Woods. *Blessed Mother Theodore Guerin. Her Journey of Faith and Courage.* (DVD). Saint Mary-of-the-Woods: Sisters of Providence, 1999.

Wilkes, C. Gene. *Jesus on Leadership.* Wheaton, IL: Tyndale House Publishers, Inc., 1998.

Acknowledgments

The Sisters of Providence of Saint Mary-of-the-Woods, Indiana—especially Sister Marie Kevin Tighe, Sister Mary Roger Madden, Sister Mary Catherine Livers, Sister Mary Ryan, Sister Marianne Mader, and Sister Ruth Eileen Dwyer—have my deepest gratitude for their warm hospitality and assistance with information, documentation, interviews and resources in writing this book. In addition, my many thanks to three of my former professors from Saint Mary-of-the-Woods College whom I call friends and mentors: Sister Alexa Suelzer, the Reverend Bernard LaMontagne, and Dr. Virginia Unverzagt. Their input in this book was very helpful. I also appreciate Mr. Philip McCord for his time and accessibility in sharing his story with me.

The pastor of Saint Peter Church, the Reverend Monsignor Joseph Jarmoluk, and the parochial vicar, Reverend Bruce Ludeke, have my deepest gratitude for their spiritual guidance, as well as Reverend Max Lasrado, formerly a parochial vicar at Saint Peter's.

Publisher Greg Pierce, editor L. C. Fiore, and the rest of the team at ACTA Publications are a pleasure to work with. I thank them for their professionalism, expertise and kindness. I also thank my sister, Patricia Doyle Brewer, and my daughter, Erin Cannella, for periodically reading rough copies of the manuscript in the book's early stages. I greatly appreciate their time and comments. I also thank my husband, Marshall Brodien, for his love and support as well as the rest of my family and close friends. I am richly blessed.